Portrait of César Franck by Mlle. Jeanne Rongier

[From the catalogue of the Exhibition at the
Palais des Champs Elysées, 1 May 1888.]

Toward an Authentic Interpretation of the Organ Works of César Franck

by Rollin Smith

PENDRAGON PRESS  *New York*

The Juilliard Performance Guides
A Scholarly Series for the Practical Musician

Library of Congress Cataloging in Publication Data

Smith, Rollin.
     Toward an authentic interpretation of the organ works
of César Franck.

   (Juilliard performance guides; no. 1)
     1. Franck, César, Organ music. 2. Organ music— —
Interpretation (Phrasing, dynamics, etc.) I. Titles.
II. Series.
ML410.F82S6   1983   786.5'092'4   83-8273
ISBN 0-918728-25-8

CONTENTS

ILLUSTRATIONS

ACKNOWLEDGEMENTS

A debt of gratitude is acknowledged to those who assisted me during the research, preparation and writing of this study:

Barry Brook, my doctoral adviser, for his patience, insight and generous guidance;

André Marchal, who replied to certain questions relative to the original organ of the Basilica of Sainte-Clotilde;

Flor Peeters, who provided the measurements of the original console of the organ of Sainte-Clotilde;

Fenner Douglass, Jean-Louis Coignet and Kurt Lueders, for their advice, comments and endless supply of information regarding French organs;

Richard Warren, Director of Yale University's Historical Sound Recordings Collection, who spent several hours playing and discussing the recordings of Charles Tournemire;

Rachelle Knapp, for her knowledgeable supervision of the French translations;

Terry Eason, for the diagram on page 56;

Charles Henderson, for his extensive and valuable editorial assistance and suggestions for the presentation of the subject;

Robert Price, who edited and typed the final manuscript;

Anthony Baglivi, who initiated, stimulated and shared my enthusiasm for the music of César Franck. His encouragement and critical analysis of the various drafts determined the progress of this work.

LEGEND

The designation of pitches throughout this book follows the "Plaine and Easie Code." Commas or apostrophes preceding the pitch name identify the octave placement of that pitch.

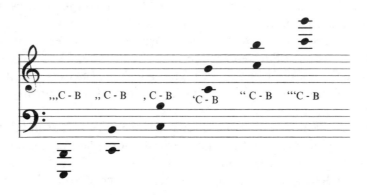

from
Barry S. Brook, "The simplified plaine and easie code system for notating music, a proposal for international adoption," *Fontes Artis Musicae*, XXI/2–3 (May–Sept. 1965) 156–60.

INTRODUCTION

If a composer's greatness could be judged by the amount of critical study of his life and works César Franck's stature would be assured. A respected church organist for almost fifty years, a noted performer and composer, and, as professor of organ at the Paris Conservatoire, the teacher of a wide circle of distinguished musicians, Franck has been the subject of innumerable books, monographs and articles. But throughout this extensive bibliography, no comprehensive work which deals specifically with his career as an organist and organ teacher can be found.

After more than one hundred years, Franck's organ works have triumphantly passed Dr. Johnson's test: ". . . length of duration and continuance of esteem." His twelve major organ works enjoy a popularity which surpasses even that of his *Symphony in D minor*. To the music world in general the concept of César Franck as organist and undisputed master of nineteenth-century French organ composition pervades nearly every reference to his works in other media.

Since Franck's death in 1890, many scholars and performers, while providing increasingly subjective interpretations of his organ works, claimed to have learned a "truc" style of playing his music from a teacher who "inherited the tradition" from the master himself. The music gradually assumed, within a few decades, a self-indulgent stamp at one extreme and a self-styled "aristocratic" interpretation at the other. Between these poles lies the "Sainte-Clotilde tradition" maintained by the successive illustrious *titulaires* of Franck's church. The traditions which have developed around Franck and the organ have, like those of Bach and Liszt, obscured facts obtainable from contemporary accounts of his playing and from the music itself.

It is the purpose of this study to compile and examine the extant firsthand references to Franck as an organ student, organ player and organ teacher written by those who knew him, heard him and studied with him. We shall study the organ over which he presided for thirty years and under whose influence his organ works were composed. And we shall study the writings and recordings of his student and successor, Charles Tournemire.

It is our hope that this information will lead the serious artist nearer to an authentic interpretation of the organ works of César Franck.

Toward an Authentic Interpretation of the Organ Works of César Franck

CHAPTER ONE

CÉSAR FRANCK – ORGAN STUDENT

ॴ⟨᠊᠊⟩ॴ

César Auguste Franck was born on 10 December 1822 in Liège, Belgium. His father, a bank clerk, had decided upon a musical profession, and more specifically, a virtuoso career, for his son, and to that end, he was enrolled in the Liège Conservatoire in October 1830. There he won a first prize for solfège in 1832 and a first prize for piano in February, 1834. He also studied (probably organ) with Duguet, the blind organist of the Church of Saint-Denis.

The family immigrated to Paris in 1836 and César was admitted to the Conservatoire Nationale de Musique de Paris on 4 October 1837. That he was no ordinary fourteen-year-old student is attested to by a newspaper notice of that same year which places him ". . . on an equal commercial basis with three of the best known virtuosi of the time: the pianist Pixis, now nearing fifty, the celebrated Alkan, and the illustrious Franz Liszt."[1]

Franck studied piano with Pierre Zimmermann and fugue with Aimé-Amroise-Simon Leborne. He entered the competition for the piano prize in 1838. Because he transposed the sight-reading test a minor third below, Cherubini, the director, refused to grant him the first prize, but he did recommend a special award—the "Grand Prix d'Honneur." In October of 1840 César Franck entered the organ class of François Benoist.[2]

---

[1] Ronald Smith, *Alkan* (London: Kahn & Averill, 1976) 30.

[2] A graduate of the Paris Conservatoire, Benoist had won first prizes in harmony and piano and, in 1815 the Prix de Rome. In 1819 he was appointed organist of the Royal Chapel and, as a result of this prestigious position, became professor of

That same year Benoist, in addition to his responsibilities at the Conservatoire, had been appointed chorus-master at l'Opéra. Saint-Saëns gives us a glimpse of the organ class in session.

> He collaborated in several ballets for the Opera and that gave him a good deal of work to do. It sounds incredible but he used to bring his "work" to class and scribble away on his orchestrations while his pupils played the organ. This in no way prevented him from hearing and supervising them or leaving his work to make the necessary criticism.[3]

The organ class was held in a small examination hall which was designed as a theater. The walls, as those in all the rooms of the Conservatoire, were painted a bluish gray, spotted with black. Massenet informs us that the two-manual *grand orgue*, an ". . . old, worn, squeaky instrument" stood at the back of the stage ". . . hidden behind a large curtain. . . ."[4]

Designed to prepare the students for the annual competition for the first prize in organ, the curriculum remained unchanged until well into the present century so that Franck studied under Benoist exactly what he himself later taught when he succeeded Benoist as professor of organ. Three of Franck's students described the class and the examination requirements:

> The tests for this examination were—and still are—four in number: the accompaniment of a plainchant chosen for the occasion, the performance

---

organ at the Conservatoire. He held this post for the next fifty-three years—so long that it was jokingly said that three republics and two empires had lived and died under him. (Laurence Davies, *César Franck and His Circle* [London: Harris & Jenkins, 1970] 76) Camille Saint-Saëns, one of Benoist's former students, described him as ". . . an excellent and charming man, familiarly known as 'Father Benoist.' He was a very ordinary organist but an admirable teacher. . . . He had little to say, but as his taste was refined and his judgment sure, nothing he said lacked weight or authority." (Camille Saint-Saëns, *Portraits et Souvenirs* [Paris: Société d'édition artistique, 1899]. Translated by Edwin Rich under the title, *Musical Memories* [Boston: Small, Maynard, 1919] 16)

Among the laureates of the organ class were such important composers as Adolphe Adam, Hector Berlioz, Camille Saint-Saëns, Georges Bizet, Léo Delibes, Félicien David and Charles Gounod; prominent organists Lefébure-Wély, Édouard Batiste (Delibes's uncle), Alexis Chauvet, Renaud de Vilbac, Théodore Salomé and Théodore Dubois; and pianists Charles-Valentin Alkan, Henri Duvernoy, and Raoul Pugno.

[3] Saint-Saëns, *Musical Memories*, 16.

[4] Jules Massenet, *Mes Souvenirs* (Paris: Lafitte, 1912). Translated by H. Villiers Barnett as *My Recollections* (Boston: Small, Maynard, 1919) 4.

of an organ piece with pedal, the improvisation of a fugue, and the improvisation of a piece in sonata form, both these improvisations being upon themes set by the examiners.[5]

The lessons were composed of . . . improvisations of plainchant, improvisations of florid counterpoint, improvisations of a sonata on a free theme and, at the end, a piece for performance.[6]

Plainsong . . . improvisation of a fugue on a given subject, free improvisation on a given theme, performance from memory of an organ piece from the great repertoire, ancient or modern—such were the other tests required for the examination and the competition.[7]

Three-quarters of the studies of the class were devoted to improvisation. Indeed, the class served not to train virtuosi but as a workshop to develop skills in improvisation for those musicians who were already exceptional players. Most of the students were also competent composers. The value of improvisation to exercise and stimulate the creative musical mind has always been stressed in France. Saint-Saëns speaks of its importance in the organist's art:

Formerly, improvisation was the basis of the organist's talent; his virtuosity was slight—music written for organ with obbligato pedal was beyond his powers. As a compensation we had improvisations of the highest order . . . . It is improvisation alone which permits one to employ all the resources of a large instrument, and to adapt oneself to the infinite variety of organs; only improvisation can follow the service perfectly, the pieces written for this purpose being almost always too short or too slow. Finally, the practice of improvisation develops faculties of invention which, without it, would have remained latent.[8]

Extramusical considerations, such as the church's liturgical demands, necessitated the study of improvisation. Joseph Bonnet describes the practical value of *extempore* playing in France:

[5] Vincent d'Indy, *César Franck* (Paris: Alcan, 1906) trans. Rosa Newmarch (London: John Lane The Bodley Head, 1909) 33.

[6] Pierre de Lapommeraye, "César Franck Intime: Une conversation avec M. Gabriel Pierné," *Le Ménestrel* (Dec. 1922) 484.

[7] Louis Vierne, *Mes Souvenirs*, first published as a series of articles in *L'Orgue* (Paris, Sept. 1934 to Sept. 1937). Translated by Esther E. Jones as "Memoirs of Louis Vierne: His Life and Contacts with Famous Men," *The Diapason* (Sept. 1938 to Sept. 1939). Page references pertain to the collected edition (Paris: Les Amis de l'Orgue, 1970) 23.

[8] Camille Saint-Saëns, "Music in the Church," *The Musical Quarterly* II/1 (Jan. 1916) 8.

No one may keep a position in any Catholic church in France without being a very able improviser. The part the organ plays in the Roman French ritual is so elaborate that the organist is relieved of any accompaniment of the choir. In addition to the grand organ, generally placed in the west gallery, there is always a chancel organ, and another organist or choirmaster is in charge of the choir. On the grand organ are played not only the preludes, offertories and postludes, which may be taken from written music, but also a great number of more or less developed interludes for which only improvisation is possible.

Take, for example, the vesper service: it includes the singing of five psalms, a hymn and the Magnificat. At the end of each psalm, after the repeating of the antiphon, the organist plays an interlude related to the melody of the psalm or of the antiphon. Between verses of the hymn and of the Magnificat the same procedure is followed. Now, you could hardly make any choirmaster give you the keys in which these chants will be sung. They may vary in pitch from half a tone to one-and-a-half tones. Most of the time the choirmaster plays his accompaniments to the Gregorian chants *extempore*. Furthermore, during the Magnificat, the priest, deacon and sub-deacon proceed to the incensing of the altar, of the clergy in the sanctuary and, afterwards, of the congregation. The length of this ritual may vary and the organist must see that the singing of the Doxology, which comes at the end of the incensing, is in accord with the singing of the choir. In view of this, one must realize the great necessity for fluent improvisation.[9]

To develop facility in handling counterpoint in improvisation a style of accompanying Gregorian chant had been invented. Two examples may be found in Appendix A. Louis Vierne describes how it was taught:

Existing since the foundation of the class in organ, it consisted in a note-for-note accompaniment of a liturgical chant in the upper part; then the chant became the bass in whole notes, not transposed, accompanied by three upper parts in a sort of classical florid counterpoint; the whole notes then passed into the top part, transposed a fourth higher, and received in their turn the classical florid accompaniment. Nothing was closer to formula than this counterpoint, strict without being exactly so, crammed with retarded fifths, with seventh chords prolonged with the fifth, with sequences—in a word, with all that is forbidden in written

---

[9] Joseph Bonnet, "Bonnet shows how a church in France selects an organist," extract of a speech given at a dinner of the Guilmant Organ School Alumni Association, New York City, 19 Oct. 1942, *The Diapason* (Dec. 1942) 7.

counterpoint. . . . In those bygone days one did not hesitate to accompany each note with a chord, an effect about as artistic as if it were applied to the vocal runs of *bel canto.*[10]

A record of the organ literature studied by the students of Benoist's class does not exist. Standards of organ playing were low and although the organ works of Bach were not unknown, it is said that Paris might have been searched "in vain to find two organists who knew the *Fugue in B minor*"[11] The first volume of Bach's complete organ works was not published until 1844[12] —two years after Franck had left the Conservatoire. Jean-Bonaventure Laurens, commenting on the unavailability of Bach's organ music, then obtainable only from foreign sources, wrote:

> . . . no publisher has ever found himself encouraged to engrave and print a single line of these organ works since they all demand the use of the pedals, a technical feat that practically no one in this country seems at the moment to have mastered.[13]

After one year in the organ class, César Franck competed for the First Prize on 21 July.

> Franck, with his wonderful instinct for counterpoint, observed that the subject given for the fugue lent itself to combination with that of the free composition, and treated them simultaneously, in such a way that one set off the other.
> He tells us that he was "very successful in combining the two subjects," but the developments which grew out of this unusual method of treating the free composition ran to such unaccustomed lengths that the examiners, bewildered by such a technical feat, awarded nothing. . . .[14]

It was only through Benoist's intervention that the jury grudgingly

[10] Vierne, *Mes Souvenirs,* 22.

[11] Charles Marie Widor, "Preface," to *L'Orgue de J. S. Bach* by André Pirro (Paris: Fischbacher, 1895) trans. Wallace Goodrich (New York: Schirmer, 1902) xix.

[12] This was the C. F. Peters edition. See Albert Riemenschneider and Herman Keller, "A short history of the basic Griepenkerl edition of Bach's organ works," *Eighth Music Book*, ed. Max Hinrichsen (London: Hinrichsen, 1956) 138. The first volume of the Bach-Gesellschaft edition of the organ works did not appear until 1865.

[13] *Revue et Gazette musicale de Paris* (2 Nov. 1845) 362.

[14] d'Indy, *Franck,* 34.

awarded Franck the Second Prize (a copy of Rossini's *Guillaume Tell*!).[15]

After one more semester, Franck's father withdrew him from the Conservatoire in the spring of 1842 and the family returned to Liège. Two years of futile attempts to establish a career as composer and piano virtuoso followed. The Franck family migrated back to Paris where César supported himself by teaching piano, privately at his small apartment at 69 rue Blanche, at Collège Rollin (a school for young girls at Auteuil), and at Collège des Jésuites de Vaugirard.[16]

[15] Norman Demuth, *César Franck* (New York: Philosophical Library, 1949) 21.

[16] Jean Gallois, *César Franck* (Paris: Editions du Seuil, 1966) 56.

Franck at 24 in 1846

Notre-Dame-de-Lorette, Nave

CHAPTER TWO

CÉSAR FRANCK – ORGANIST

᪲ᘛ᪲ᘚ᪲

It was not as a composer but as an organist that César Franck's musical reputation was established among his contemporaries. Georges Bizet, upon hearing the *Prélude, Fugue et Variation*, exclaimed, "Your piece is exquisite. I did not know you were a composer, too!"[1]

Even Franck's organ students were unfamiliar with his composi tions. Charles Tournemire, during a lesson at Sainte-Clotilde, was asked by Franck, "Do you know *Rédemption?*"

"What, Gounod's work?"

"No," replied Franck, "mine. Have a look at it and you will see that it is altogether a better work than the one you mentioned."[2]

As a composer Franck did not mature until his mid-fifties. As an organist he had played, since his thirties, in the inaugural recital of practically every important organ in the French capital.[3] And we shall see as we review his public performances, the esteem and admiration in which he was held by all of the musicians and critics of his time.

[1] Charles Tournemire, *César Franck* (Paris: Delagrave, 1931) 72.

[2] *Ibid.*

[3] He was associated, on a professional basis, with the church of Notre-Dame-de-Lorette from the early 1840's, but we know nothing of his duties except that he was "organiste accompagnateur." (Gallois, *Franck*, 59) Gallois (*Ibid.*, 58) mentions that in 1845 Franck dedicated an *Ave Maria* to the curé of the parish in the hope of one day obtaining the post of maître de chapelle.

The orgue-de-choeur, a two-manual instrument built by Somer, had been brought from the old chapelle Saint-Jean-Porte-Latine to the new church in 1836. (Félix Raugel, "Les orgues de Notre-Dame-de-Lorette de Paris," *L'Orgue* No. 111 [July–Sept. 1964] 88).

In 1851 Abbé Dancel, the vicar of Notre-Dame-de-Lorette, was transferred to

Franck at 30 in 1852

The first mention of César Franck as an organist in public recital is a notice of the inauguration of the new Ducroquet organ at the church of Saint-Eustache. Franck played on 26 May 1854, in company with a fellow Belgian, Nicolas-Jacques Lemmens, and two Parisian organists: Carvallo and Bazille. (It was customary throughout the nineteenth century to have new organs inaugurated not by one artist, but by as many prominent organists as could be assembled for the occasion. Thus, the most famous names in French organ music often appear on the same program, each playing a piece and/or an improvisation.) On this program "César Franck played a fantaisie composed with care and energetically performed."[4]

On 30 August 1856, Franck demonstrated the organ for the Cathedral of Carcassonne in the erecting room of the Cavaillé-Coll organ factory.

> The interpreter, César Franck, an excellent organist, highlighted all the riches and harmonic resources, first by a knowledgeable execution of "severe" music, very well written by himself, and then by brilliant improvisations.[5]

Sometime in the late fall of 1857 Franck assumed the duties of "maître de chapelle et premier organiste de la paroisse de Sainte-Clotilde."[6] Services were held in a temporary chapel, Sainte-Valère, in the rue de Bourgogne until the new church was opened

Dedicated in honor of Sainte-Clotilde on 30 November 1857, this basilica was the first large neo-Gothic church to be built in France.[7] Franck presided at a small organ, first in the chapel and then in the

---

the Marais parish of Saint-Jean-Saint-François and took Franck with him as organist. At this church Cavaillé-Coll's 1844 Exposition organ had been reinstalled. (Félix Raugel, *Les Grandes Orgues des Églises de Paris* [Paris: Fischbacher, 1927] 181) Franck was so enchanted with the sonorities of the modest 2-manual, 18-stop organ that, when asked about it, he exclaimed, "My new organ? It is an orchestra!" (Davies, *Franck and His Circle*, 73).

[4] *Revue et Gazette musicale de Paris* (21 May 1854) 175.

[5] *Revue et Gazette musicale de Paris* (30 August 1856) 248. Because this notice is identical to those appearing in other journals, Léon Vallas conjectures that this was a press release supplied by Cavaillé-Coll himself. (Léon Vallas, *La véritable histoire de César Franck* [Paris: Flammarion, 1950]. Translated by Hubert Foss as *César Franck* [New York: Oxford University Press, 1951] 109).

[6] Gallois, *Franck*, 64.

[7] Armin Landgraf, *Musica Sacra zwischen Symphonie und Improvisation: César Franck und seine Musik fur den Gottesdienst* (Tutzing: Schneider, 1975) 47.

Saint-Jean-Saint-François, Nave

Kurt Lueders

new building. In December 1859 the new organ, destined to be one of Cavaillé-Coll's most famous instruments, was dedicated. At this organ Franck's activities as composer, organist and improviser became legendary. Here his twelve monuments of romantic organ literature were conceived and executed.

For the dedication of his own organ at Sainte-Clotilde on 19 December 1859, Franck was joined by Lefébure-Wély. At this time Franck played two of the *Six Pièces* (one of which was the *Final*, Op. 21, dedicated to Lefébure-Wély), as well as improvisations and Bach's *Prelude and Fugue in E minor*.

> M. Franck, organist of the parish, began with a piece of his own written in a broad and forceful style which made a deep impression on his hearers who also appreciated M. Franck when he turned from his own compositions to draw on those conceived by the genius of Sebastian Bach. . . . Serious studies such as these reveal in him a perserverence and give him, at present, a place among organists of the first order. He showed himself at his best when, resuming his rôle as composer, he played his *Final* on the full organ. In this *Final* one recognized the conception and execution of a true master.[8]

The inauguration of the largest organ in France, the Cavaillé-Coll of Saint-Sulpice, on 29 April 1862, brought together César Franck, Camille Saint-Saëns and Alexandre Guilmant (a twenty-five-year-old organist from Boulogne-sur-Mer who would one day be Franck's second successor as organ professor at the Conservatoire). A notice read that "M. Franck was severe without pedantry; and M. Saint-Saëns, profound without obscurity."[9]

On Monday evening, 26 April 1863, the organ of Saint-Étienne-du-Mont, rebuilt by Cavaillé-Coll, was opened by several artists, including César Franck who ". . . made masterly use of the 16' and 8' foundation stops.[10]

At Sainte-Clotilde, on the evening of 17 November 1864, Franck played a concert of his own compositions which included the complete *Six Pièces.*

[8] *Revue et Gazette musicale de Paris* (1 Jan. 1860) 4. "M. Franck played, among other pieces in a grave style, a fugue of Bach and a remarkable *Offertoire* of his own composition." ("Nouvelles Diverses," *Le Ménestrel* [25 Dec. 1859] 31).

[9] *Ibid.* (11 May 1862) 155. Louis Roger, after writing in *Revue de musique sacrée* that Guilmant's *Méditation* "recalled the naïve grace of Haydn," reproached M. Franck for playing too long! (Alexandre Cellier et Henri Bachelin, *L'Orgue* [Paris: Delagrave, 1933] 185).

[10] *Revue et Gazette musicale de Paris* (3 May 1863) 143.

Franck at 40 in 1862

Franck at 35 in 1857

M. César Franck gave a recital last Thursday at Sainte-Clotilde which was attended by a large number of artists and music lovers. Franck's compositions, written by the hand of a master, were played by him. One notices in the first the happiest effect of a choir of *Voix humaines*; and in the *Grande Pièce symphonique* a most distinguished melody played first on the Clarinet and later repeated on the *Voix célestes*. At this concert M. Franck showed himself to be as learned a composer as he is a skillful instrumentalist and will have proved one more time that the standards of French organists are being raised day by day.[11]

On 13 April 1866, Franck gave another recital at his church which was attended by Franz Liszt. The Weimar Master had previously attended Mass at Sainte-Clotilde and had congratulated Franck on his improvisations.[12] It may have been at this concert that Liszt exclaimed: "These poems have their place beside the masterpieces of Sebastian Bach."[13]

The published account of this concert follows:

The various compositions played by M. Franck, conceived in a very severe style which, not excluding variety, made marvellous use of the numerous resources of the organ of Sainte-Clotilde, one of Cavaillé-Coll's best instruments. Liszt, in whose honor this recital was given, complimented M. Franck on the elevated style of his works and his magisterial execution.[14]

Franck, Alexis Chauvet, Auguste Durand and P. Serrier inaugurated the Cavaillé-Coll organ at Saint-Denis-du-Saint-Sacrament on 10 October 1867.[15]

[11] *Revue et Gazette musicale de Paris* (20 Nov. 1864) 375.

[12] Alexandre de Bertha, who had gone with his teacher, Franz Liszt, to hear Franck and Lefébure-Wély in 1866, wrote: "As a matter of fact, neither one nor the other pleased us, considering the subtlety of the first and the affectation of the second, little in keeping with the grandiose character of their instrument." ("Franz Liszt," *Bulletin français de la S. I. M.* [1907] 1163. Quoted in "L'art des organistes" by André Pirro in *Encyclopédie de la Musique et Dictionnaire du Conservatoire, Deuxième Partie* [Paris: Delagrave, 1926] 1371).

[13] d'Indy, *Franck*, 137. D'Indy says elsewhere (*Ibid.*, 44) that is was on 3 April 1866 that "Franz Liszt, who had been his sole listener, left the church of Sainte-Clotilde lost in amazement, and evoking the name of J. S. Bach in inevitable comparison."

[14] *Revue et Gazette musicale de Paris* (22 April 1866) 126.

[15] Raugel, *Les Grandes Orgues de Paris*, 177.

The new organ of Notre-Dame Cathedral was dedicated by an illustrious group of organists on Friday, 6 March 1868, at eight o' clock in the evening. Saint-Saëns, Guilmant and Widor[16] all played their own works. Franck played his *Fantaisie*, Op. 16.[17]

The 45-stop organ at La Trinité was inaugurated on 16 March 1869.

> M. César Franck of Sainte-Clotilde played a vigorous well-developed improvisation in which he sought to point up the greatest possible number of sonorities.[18]

Years later Charles Marie Widor recalled that ". . . the themes, their development and execution were equally admirable: he never wrote better!"[19]

At the Third Programme of the Societé des Concerts du Conservatoire in January 1873, "César Franck, the eminent organist, was applauded for the severe beauties of a *Prelude and Fugue in E minor* for organ of J. S. Bach."[20] Two months later, on 11 March "César Franck improvised on the organ with his usual talent"[21] in the Salle de Conservatoire at a concert of the Société Chorale d'Amateurs.

On Tuesday afternoon, 1 October 1878, at three o'clock in the afternoon Franck played the 14th Séance de l'Orgue in the Salle des Fêtes of the Trocadéro.[22] The program, as advertised in advance, read:

> Fantaisie
> Grande Pièce symphonique
> Cantabile

[16] Guilmant and Widor had been heard together previously at the inauguration of the Cavaillé-Coll organ at the Carmelite Church, Kensington, London 15 July 1866.

[17] *Revue et Gazette musicale de Paris* (18 March 1868) 85.

[18] *Ibid.* (16 March 1869) 101.

[19] Raugel, *Les Grandes Orgues de Paris*, 220. Franck was familiar with other organs than those built by Cavaillé-Coll. For instance, in 1871 he served with Théodore Dubois on a commission which received the new organ at Saint-Paul-Saint-Louis. The three-manual, 36-stop instrument was built by Martin of Rouen.

[20] *Revue et Gazette musicale de Paris* (5 Jan. 1873) 5.

[21] *Ibid.* (26 April 1873) 85.

[22] The Palais du Trocadéro was a bizarre Oriental palace built for the Universal Exhibition of 1878. The large semicircular slope on which it stood, and the square behind it, were renamed the Trocadéro in memory of a Spanish fort by that name, near Cadiz, which was captured in 1823 by the French army under the Duc d'Angoulême. (Harold P. Clunn, *The Face of Paris* [London: Spring Books, c. 1960] 137).

> Improvisation on themes of French masters:
>   Berlioz, David, Bizet
> Pièce héroïque
> Improvisation on Russian, Hungarian, Irish
>   Scottish and Swedish themes[23]

This, in its entirety, is the review of the concert:

The recital given by M. C. Franck summed up, so to speak, the man himself: composer, improvisateur and executant, and, with the authority of a master, he proved himself equal to the entire program. Three new and unpublished works of his own composition have been heard for the first time at this performance. The *Fantasia en la* is a beautiful piece, very skillfully wrought; but all the details were not brought out well, the soft stops lacking presence and distinctness in the hall. The *Cantabile in B major*, an impressive melody of noble character was more effective thanks to the telling *Récit* stop employed. The *Pièce héroïque,* although containing some excellent things seemed less interesting than the two other works. As for the *Grande Pièce symphonique in F-sharp minor*, it has long been known and justly appreciated; the *andante*, as always, was warmly welcomed. In his program M. Franck had devoted a large part to improvisation for which all real musicians had to be grateful. His free-style treatment of themes of Félicien David (first chorus from *Le Désert*), Berlioz (two motifs from *L'Enfance du Christ*), Bizet (two motifs from *L'Arlésienne*), created charming details. He was particularly successful with Berlioz' themes. At the end he returned again to that interesting part of the organist's art, by improvising on Russian themes (two pretty popular motifs), first treated separately, then superimposed, Swedish, Hungarian and English themes. The motifs were too numerous and it would not have been possible to take advantage of each one sufficiently without fatiguing the audience. With this slight reservation, we are happy to pay homage to the most elevated and the most complete talent we know. We have congratulated ourselves once more that such a peerless artist is at the head of organ teachers in France.[24]

For the inauguration of the renovated organ at Saint-Merry on 10 November 1878, "M. Wachs, organiste titulaire, Franck and Gigout played some beautiful pages of Bach, Mendelssohn, and Boëly."[25]

On Thursday, 29 February 1879, on the new tubular-pneumatic organ built by the firm of Fermis & Persil for Saint-François-Xavier,

[23] *Revue et Gazette musicale de Paris* (29 Sept. 1878) 313–14.
[24] *Revue et Gazette musicale de Paris* (6 Oct. 1878) 321.
[25] *Ibid.* (10 Nov. 1878) 367.

"Franck, Widor, Gigout, and Albert Renaud played several of their own works."[26]

In 1879 at Saint-Eustache a new Merklin organ replaced the Ducroquet organ which Franck had dedicated twenty-five years before. Among the committee of experts controlling the restoration were Franck, Guilmant, Dubois, and Gigout. These same four men played on the inaugural program on 21 March.

> . . . M. C.-A. Franck, organist of Sainte-Clotilde and professor of organ at the Conservatoire, was heard in his beautiful *Fantaisie en la*; designated on the program under the title *Cantabile*, a well-developed piece of great elevation of style, full of rich ideas and new details. This *Fantaisie* has already been played with great success at the concert given by the composer at the Trocadéro.[27]

Franck lived in the parish of Saint-Jacques-du-Haut-Pas and in 1889 Merklin installed an organ with electric action in the church.[28] (Franck's brother, Joseph, had been organist there in the late 1860's.) One two-manual organ was in the choir and another two-manual organ was in the west gallery. The two organs, each comprising a Grand-Orgue and Récit, were almost identical and were controlled by a four-manual console in the sanctuary. Franck always showed an interest in this "modern" organ and played at the blessing on 27 May, ". . . from the common console, playing the two organs alternately and together with satisfaction."[29]

---

[26] *Ibid.* (9 March 1879) 78. Franck played his *Cantabile* and Eugène Gigout played the *Final* of a *Concerto in G minor* of Handel. (Norbert Dufourcq, *Eugène Gigout* [Paris: L'Orgue, Cahiers et Mémoires, No. 27, 1982] 6).

[27] *Revue et Gazette musicale de Paris* (30 March 1879) 101.

[28] The year before, Merklin had built a fifteen-stop orgue-de-choeur at Sainte-Clotilde. In fact, it immediately precedes that of Saint-Jacques-du-Haut-Pas on the *Liste des Orgues Électroniques de la Maison J. Merklin* [Paris] 1891. Audsley singles out this instrument of Sainte-Clotilde as an ". . . unusual disposition of the Choir Organ. Here it is divided into two sections of equal size, and placed, in elevated positions, in the side arches of the apsidal sanctuary, in line with the steps to the high altar. The console is located at the end of the stalls on the left side as one faces the altar. The organ is electro-pneumatic, and the bellows are placed immediately behind the high altar. This arrangement proves very satisfactory." (George Ashdown Audsley, *The Art of Organ Building, Vol. I* [New York: Dodd, Mead & Co., 1905] 95) Because this organ no longer exists this digression may be of interest to our readers.

[29] G. Blondel, *Rapport sur le grand orgue de tribune et l'orgue de choeur de l'église Saint-Jacques-du-Haut-Pas à Paris* (Paris, 1908) See *Le Ménestrel* (19 May 1889) 160.

References to Franck as an improviser become plentiful and elaborate when we move from the concert settings to the subdued ecclesiastical atmosphere of the Basilica of Sainte-Clotilde where he played the organ ". . . every Sunday and feast day—and towards the end of his life every Friday morning. . . ."[30]

Vincent d'Indy summed up Franck's talent in relation to the other organists of the day:

> Franck had, or rather *was* the genius of improvisation and no other modern organist, not excepting the most renowned executants, would bear the most distant comparison with him in this respect.[31]

That Franck's playing was on an extraordinarily elevated plane impressed his students:

> . . . a remarkable organist, full of love for his instrument and careful to avoid degrading it as do, alas! too many of his fellows, to the poor art of entertainer of the swarming crowds that fill the churches.[32]

Louis Vierne wrote:

> I have never heard anything which could compare with the purely musical invention of Franck's improvisations. At church it took him a certain time to get into the mood—several trials, a little experimenting, then once started, a lavishness of invention partaking of the miraculous, a polyphony of incomparable richness, in which melody, harmony and structure vied with one another in originality and emotional conception, traversed by flashes of manifest genius. Never any combinations just for their own sake, never any feats of skill customary among the acrobats desirous of dazzling the gallery; only a constant concern for the dignity of his art, for the nobility of his mission, for the fervent sincerity of his sermon in sound. Joyous or melancholy, solemn or mystic, powerful or

---

[30] d'Indy, *Franck*, 42.

[31] d'Indy, *Franck*, 43. D'Indy's opinion was shared by the American virtuoso, Clarence Eddy, who had heard Franck extemporize in 1890 and considered him "one of the greatest masters among the French organists. . . . His improvisations were a marvel—something unique." (Clarence Eddy, "Leading organists of France and Italy," *Music* [Dec. 1896] 166).

[32] J. Guy Ropartz, "César Franck," *Revue Internationale de Musique* (13 June 1898). Translated by Miss Milman in *Studies in Music by Various Authors*, reprinted from *The Musician*, ed. Robin Grey (London: Simpkin, Marshall, Hamilton, Kent and Co., 1901) 108. Franck is said to have replied to those who criticized his "severe" style: "I am sorry to not please everyone, but I play the organ my way." (Arment Vivet, "Eugène Gigout," *L'Orgue et les Organistes*, No. 23 [15 Feb. 1926] 25).

ethereal, Franck knew how to be all those at Sainte-Clotilde, and mere technical resources such as contrapuntal artifices, canons, superimposition of themes, etc. would never appear except when justified by the expression of a thought whose criterion was essentially depth and emotion.[33]

The improvisation occurred after the sermon: at the Offertory, the Communion, and the end of Mass (the Sortie).

It was there that Franck was truly unique. He took a theme from one of the little notebooks[34] or asked one of his assistants to propose one. Then, the theme chosen, he would reflect before improvising; with his right elbow held in his left hand he would tap his forehead with the third finger of his right hand; and from that moment nothing existed for him but the music, and when translated to the organ, it was something unimaginable: the themes linking themselves in logical continuity, with a correctness, an unheard-of facility and all taking on an aspect of solidity of a great work.[35]

Charles Tournemire has left us an extended description of Franck, the organist of Sainte-Clotilde:

Franck's devoted auditors, few in number, but receptive, have been able to retain extraordinary impressions: a constantly elevated style, going impeccably by the rules from a simple verset of a few measures to an imposing fresco.[36]
The *"grande fantaisie"* was often adopted; the sonata-allegro, the lied were honored. The themes treated were extracts from popular tunes and from classical works.[37] It also happened that the improvisation was based on an original theme.

---

[33] Vierne, *Mes Souvenirs*, 23.

[34] Pierné describes their contents: "Franck had little notebooks of themes which he always carried with him in the inside pocket of his frock coat. They were rectangular, one bound in black, the other in red. One contained themes of fugues that Franck collected at random from Bach, Handel, Gluck, Delibes; the subjects on one side, the answers on the other. In the red notebook were classic themes and Franck's original themes." (Lapommeraye, "César Franck Intime," 485)

[35] *Ibid.*

[36] Charles Tournemire, *Précis d'exécution, de registration et d'improvisation à l'orgue* (Paris: Eschig, 1936) 103. "Some of the scattered auditors who proceeded, tained the following impressions of the general effect of the improvisations of the composer of the *Béatitudes*."

[37] Tournemire, *Précis d'exécution*, 103. "... at this period Gregorian chant was a dead issue."

But how many times the master asked us to furnish him with some musical material to develop. The quality of the theme imposed by one of us occasionally left much to be desired ... Nevertheless, under the magician's fingers the nobility of the performance magnified its relative poverty ...

Above all it was necessary to listen to Franck at his best. Beethoven often inspired him: he was then magnificent and sometimes as beautiful as the model.[38]

The sublime constant is humanly impossible! No genius, in whatever sphere he may be, has known this grace: evenness in conception.

Our *grand musicien* was only human.

We hasten to add that his musical substance was always extraordinarily rich. In moments of relative void when the artist "searches" we waited patiently until the divine inspiration illumined his thoughts.

We rarely waited in vain ... Oh! the joys we felt at the many ways in which art manifested itself—mystical caresses, impetuous thrusts toward a lofty ideal, interior contemplation, unfathomable abysses. It was all there in those days.

How beneficent this externalization of genius tending to raise itself towards regions where all is light and peace.

The theme was rarely exposed in its entirety when he was concerned with developing it at length.

A long prelude, not precisely defined, unfolded quietly. Sometimes, even, vague figuration overlapping from one keyboard to another. The inconsistent fragments would always end up fitting together. Thus were we present at the progressive construction of polyphonic ensemble of the highest interest—a sort of *parvis* of temple.

One of the forms which we have already mentioned was chosen at the last moment; by it we were given the means of penetrating the illumined interior of this temple. Solemn moment!

With what emotion would we not await the climax of the edifying sonorous structure. Suddenly, it burst and it was truly delightful to feel its radiance.

We felt a sensation of fullness and, furthermore, we learned a significant philosophical lesson because Franck gave us the flower of his expressive soul.

During the thirty years that one of the heirs of the poetry of the Middle Ages spent at Sainte-Clotilde (from 38 to 68—the end of his life) he somehow prepared his great works on the organ.

Each Sunday this great man's mind and heart were particularly active:

---

[38] d'Indy (*Franck*, 43) remembered "... a certain offertory based upon the initial theme of Beethoven's seventh *Quartet* which nearly equaled in beauty the work of the Bonn master himself."

music improvised for the glorification of the Christian ideal was realized; perfection of order almost always attained; extremely aroused sensitivity maintained. Consequently, one understands the powerful aid brought to the work about to be written; somehow, a work preceding the latent state from whence a particular power supporting the conceptions which will later have to be committed to paper . . .

Cerebral suppleness, quick eye of the "architect-poet," coloration of ideas, organ improvisation develops these faculties.

Special ambiance, admirably suited to blooming of meditative art.[39]

Further corroboration is given by John Hinton:

He would study a subject closely for a few moments, his countenance assuming such visible signs of intensity as will not readily be forgotten by those who have seen him, and then, as it were, would "let himself go."

"I did not do this, or that." "I haven't done quite what I intended." —or, rarely, "Well, I think I have succeeded pretty well this time."

These extemporary voluntaries came to be both a pleasure and an *artistic duty* to him and, if he did not quite realize what he desired, or if the warning bell rang for him to stop just as he was piling up a closing *stretto*, he could be visibly pained and seemingly formed the resolution to "get his own back" next time by still greater concentration of energy.[40]

Of the lost improvisations Guy Ropartz lamented:

. . . had anyone noted them down Art would have been the richer by a series of compositions as finely constructed as those which he so long thought over, so carefully wrote down.[41]

Franck's use of the organ's sonorities is mirrored in the printed indications of his music. Hinton comments that his registrations at the organ of Sainte-Clotilde were

. . . sober . . . and in no degree intended to captivate the general public. But while the modern resources of the organ were not neglected by him, it is unquestionable that beauty in the design and combination of ideas, not variety in color display, was his principal quest.[42]

---

[39] Tournemire, *Franck*, 52–54.

[40] John W. Hinton, *César Franck: Some Personal Reminiscences* (London: Reeves, 1912) 12.

[41] Ropartz, *Franck*, 108.

[42] Hinton, *Franck*, 12.

Charles Tournemire gives a very detailed account of Franck's use of the organ:

> The registration of the composer of the *Three Chorals* was decorative; he used the Positif with the Récit coupled to it a great deal. By means of the swell box, the Récit foundation stops, Hautbois and Trompette harmonique coupled at unison and sub-octave pitch to the Positif 16' Bourdon, he obtained the effect of great full swell: an effect which, under his fingers, was frequently dramatic.
>
> He did not overdo the *fff* and willingly paraphrased the end of a Mass quietly.
>
> He treated the foundation stops of the coupled manuals grandly by sustaining their sumptuous harmonies.
>
> If he felt it necessary to reinforce the sonority he subtly added the mixtures and reeds in such a way so as not to disturb the tranquility of the sound but to fill it with grandeur.
>
> When using a solo stop, usually the Clarinette of the Positif or the Trompette harmonique of the Récit, one could expect some contrapuntal work of great interest on the other manual. The Clarinette which served him frequently, undoubtedly because of the extreme beauty of its timbre, was invariably accompanied by the foundation stops and Trompette of the Récit. This combination is explained thusly: the unusual intensity of this stop and the impossibility of rendering it expressive— hence the necessity of enveloping it.[43] He never abused the Voix humaine but used it with delight with the Gambe and Voix céleste coupled to the 16' Bourdon of the Positif.
>
> Profound effects attracted him. His thoughts, serious and soul-searching, sought out many full-toned combinations. He rarely confided his inspirations to the Flûte harmonique or the upper octaves of the 8' Bourdon.[44]

FRANCK AND THE CONTEMPORARY ORGAN SCENE

Franck had grown up with the "classic" organ. He played it as it evolved into the symphonic organ. He was familiar with all the different kinds of actions: mechanical (with and without Barker levers), tubular-pneumatic, and even electric action. All three churches in

---

[43] Elsewhere (*Précis*, 104), Tournemire has described the tone of this Clarinette as harsh, adding that, when Franck drew it, he "drowned" ("noyait") it with the Trompette, Hautbois, and Bourdon of the Récit.

[44] Tournemire, *Franck*, 54–55.

which he served as organist had new organs of the latest design: Cavaillé-Coll's symphonic organs—and he was completely satisfied with them. He told the curé of Sainte-Clotilde: "If you only knew how I love this instrument: it is so supple beneath my fingers and so obedient to all my thoughts!"[45]

As a performer Franck is known to have played (at least in public) only one work of J. S. Bach; yet he was thoroughly familiar with Bach's music and had many opportunities to hear his contemporaries' performances. He may have heard the German Adolph Hesse play Bach's *Toccata in F* at the inauguration of the organ of Saint-Eustache in 1844;[46] he certainly heard Guilmant play it at the same church in 1879 when they played together at the inauguration of the Merklin organ.[47]

He heard the *Prelude and Fugue in E minor*, BWV 548, played at least twice: by Lemmens at Saint-Eustache in 1854[48] and Clément Loret at Notre-Dame-de-Paris in 1868.[49]

No doubt he attended some of the Charles-Valentin Alkan's pedal-piano concerts when he played "a great part of the organ literature (including all the works of Bach)."[50] Franck and Alkan were friends: Franck called him the "Poet of the Piano"[51] and dedicated the *Grande Pièce symphonique* to him.

Franck twice played on organ inauguration concerts with, and dedicated his first major organ work to, Alexis Chauvet who was nick-named "Le petit père Bach" because he played more Bach than any other Parisian organist. Franck was interested in Alexandre Boëly, known as "The French Bach." He "was clear-sighted enough to find inspiration in him, to play his works often, and to recommend them to others."[52] His students at the Conservatoire played all of the major preludes and fugues of Bach as well as music by other organ composers.

---

[45] *Souvenir du 22 octôbre 1904. A César Franck, ses disciples, ses amis, ses admirateurs* (Paris: Cabasson, 1904) Address by Canon Gardey.

[46] *Revue et Gazette musicale de Paris* (7 July 1844) 231.

[47] Abbé H.-J. Ply, *La Facture moderne etudiée à l'orgue de Saint-Eustache* (Lyon: Perrin et Marinet, 1880) 276.

[48] *Revue et Gazette musicale de Paris* (21 May 1854) 175.

[49] *Ibid.* (15 March 1868) 85.

[50] Joseph Bloch, *Charles-Valentin Alkan* (Privately printed, 1941) 2.

[51] d'Indy, *Franck*, 95.

[52] Amédée Gastoué, A Great French Organist, Alexandre Boëly, and His Works," *The Musical Quarterly* XXX/3 (July 1944) 336.

Nor was he ignorant of his contemporaries' music. He shared recitals in which the major composers of nineteenth-century organ music played their own works: Saint-Saëns, Guilmant, Widor, Gigout and Bruckner.[53]

FINGERING

Further information about Franck's knowledge of the organ and organ playing comes from his own editorial markings. While not overly generous with fingering indications, he did not neglect them entirely. His piano music offers numerous examples of his own fingerings and some dozen passages in the organ music are fingered as well. The importance of these fingered passages to the interpretation of Franck's music is pointed out by Marguerite Long who felt "that a composer's own fingerings should be followed with the greatest respect. He knows, as part of the creative process, which hand position will achieve the best musical results."[54]

Franck uses the finger glissando in both non-legato and legato passages:

Grande Pièce symphonique, Allegro, m. 88

[53] A few weeks after the inauguration of the organ of Notre-Dame (1868) Anton Bruckner, who had come to France to inaugurate the organ at the church of Saint-Epvre in Nancy, passed through Paris on his way back to Vienna. During the first week of May he played a memorable recital at Notre-Dame which was attended by Franck, Auber, Gounod, and Saint-Saëns. At the end it appears he even surpassed the taste and great vigor of his playing in an improvisation in the form-of a Prélude, Fugue and Variation on a theme proposed by Alexis Chauvet. It was an unqualified success and Franck spoke of it long afterwards. (Raugel, *Les Grandes Orgues de Paris*, 93.)

[54] Reginald R. Gerig, *Famous Pianists and Their Technique* (Washington-New York: Luce, 1974) 320.

First Choral, m. 174

First Choral, m. 186

Finger crossings are the most frequently encountered fingerings. No consideration is given to the short fingers on white keys and long fingers on black keys. The thumb and fifth finger are used on black and white keys.

Prélude, Fugue et Variation: Variation , m. 28

Franck seldom divides voices from one staff to another. The following passage uses an uncomfortable fingering progression of 3-5-4-5:

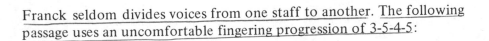

Prélude, Fugue et Variation: Fugue, m. 58

which might have been easily solved by taking the alto C♯ with the left thumb:

Prélude, Fugue et Variation: Fugue, m. 58

Although Franck did not indicate finger substitutions, he certainly used them. A passage such as the following, with the alto fingering written so that the last note is played by the thumb, presupposes finger substitution in the upper voice [bracketed fingering added by the author].

Prière, m. 179

PEDALING

Franck's other editorial markings are pedaling indications—marks denoting which toe and heel of which foot should execute which note. Before examining his "pedalings" we must investigate the evolution of his pedal technique.

It is doubtful that as a student of Benoist at the Paris Conservatoire, César Franck had acquired any facility in pedal playing. The organ examinations were played on an instrument with pedals of an octave-and-a-half range—insufficient for the literature written up to that time.

His opportunities for the exercise of a pedal technique were few after he left the Conservatoire. The range of the pedalboard of the Grand Orgue at Notre-Dame-de-Lorette was from , , C – , F (with the bottom octave extended downward three notes (, , , A – , , , A♯ – , , , B) for the reed stops. The range of the pedalboard of the organ of Saint-Jean-Saint-François was identical to that of the Conservatoire: , , C –, G. (These two organs were the only ones built by Cavaillé-Coll with less than a two-octave pedal clavier.) The organ of Sainte-Clotilde, therefore, was the first with which Franck was associated that had a pedalboard of sufficient range for the interpretation of organ literature—particularly Bach.[55]

After his performance on the organ built for the Cathedral of Carcassonne at the Cavaillé-Coll atelier in 1856, Franck may have decided that if he were to continue a public career as an organist he must accustom himself to the new extended pedalboard. So we find that shortly after his appointment to the Church of Sainte-Clotilde a Pleyel pédalier[56] was delivered to him on 28 February 1858.[57] He now had almost two years before the dedication of the new organ to acquire sufficient pedal technique to deal with two works he played at the

---

[55] The Ducroquet organ of Saint-Eustache had a 30-note pedalboard: , , C – 'F. Franck had dedicated this organ in 1854 with the Belgian Jacques Lemmens who had played the *Prelude and Fugue in E minor* of Bach. From the description which appeared in *Gazette musicale*: "His feet were everywhere at once. His feet have turned themselves into hands with an agility that extended beyond his ankles," this may be identified as BWV 548. (Vallas, *Franck*, 104)

[56] A Pédalier is an organ pedalboard used in connection with an ordinary piano for pedal practice. It either has its own independent bass strings or mechanically pulls down the corresponding bass keys of the piano.

[57] Vallas, *Franck*, 114.

inauguration: his own *Final* and Bach's *Prelude and Fugue in E minor.*[58]

By 1864 Franck's pedal technique was sufficiently developed that he could play all of his *Six Pièces* at a concert at Sainte-Clotilde.[59]

Franck has indicated pedaling in only three places: six notes in the *Pièce héroïque* and two pedal scales in an organ arrangement he made of Alkan's *Prière: "Dieu des Armées,"* a work originally written for harmonium.[60]

Franck utilizes the heel comfortably in an ascending B-flat major scale:

Alkan, *Prière: "Dieu des Armées,"* m. 62–63

It is his original solution to the scale. Notice its dissimilarity to the same scale pedaled by Lemmens:

[58] This also must have been BWV 548 as the review of his performance speculates that "M. Franck can only have attained such skill through long study and perseverence." (*Revue et Gazette musicale de Paris,* 1 Jan. 1860, 4) This comment would hardly have been elicited by the only other Bach prelude and fugue in the same key, BWV 533.

[59] Franck understood the function of the pedal organ and realized its potential as more than just an extension of the keyboard to be used for playing bass lines. The ear is not wearied by constant droning of the bass voice: it drops out frequently. And his works embody a broad spectrum of pedal writing. Use is made of light, pizzicato touch (in the *Prélude, Fugue et Variation*), canon (*Grande Pièce symphonique, Prière* and *Cantabile*), fugal development (*Prélude, Fugue et Variation* and *Grande Pièce symphonique*), double pedaling (*Grande Pièce symphonique:* second *Andante* and *Prière*), extended scalar passages (*Grande Pièce symphonique: Grand Choeur*), and virtuoso pedal solo writing *(Final).*

[60] Charles-Valentin Alkan, *Préludes et Prières*, Chosis et Arrangés pour l'Orgue par César Franck (Paris: Costallat, 1889).

Lemmens, Scale in B♭ major[61]

and that pedaled by Franck's student, Charles Tournemire:

Tournemire, Scale in B♭ major [62]

Whereas both Lemmens and Tournemire avoid the left foot above middle , C of the pedalboard, except on black keys, Franck divides the scale into two-note groups, alternates each foot for the first six notes and brings the left foot up into the middle octave for , F and , G.

The second example is an ascending ·G major scale beginning on , , D:

Alkan, *Prière: "Dieu des Armées,"* m. 70–71.

Lemmens plays , , G and , , A with the heel and then toe, and Tournemire plays , C with the left toe.

Franck wrote no extended scale passages in his organ music. Even in the virtuosic *Final* only two seven-note ascending figurations occur:

[61] Jacques Lemmens, *École d'orgue, Deuxième Partie: École de la pédale* (Bruxelles: Schott, 1862) 70.

[62] Tournemire, *Précis*, 34.

Final, m. 27

Final, m. 65

Composed of a leap, a turn, and five ascending notes, these examples are so different from those in which Franck indicated pedalings that no corollaries can be made. The examples do indicate that Franck made frequent use of the heel and thereby achieved a smoothness of execution.

The third example of Franck's pedaling indications, the *only* example which occurs in any of his original organ works, is in the middle of the *Pièce héroïque*:

Pièce héroïque, m. 117

The pedal has been playing a "quasi timpani" motive. The right foot being on the swell lever, the motive must be played by the left foot alone. The two notes, a minor third apart, are indicated by the composer to be played by the alternating heel and toe of the left foot. So indicated, we can assume this motive is to be played legato whenever it occurs.

HOW FRANCK PLAYED

The preceding pages attest that Franck's improvisational skill was unrivaled in an era of skilled improvisers. "Brilliant," is the word used more than once to describe his "well-developed and vigorous" improvisations. But it is the descriptions of his interpretations of composed music that is pertinent to our study.

Franck performed ten organ works in public: Bach's *Prelude and Fugue in E minor*, BWV 548, and his own *Six Pièces* and *Trois Pièces*. This is the repertoire which is described as "severe music" and as being in a "very severe style." In view of the taste of most of the organists with whom he appeared in public, those who specialized in trivialities and in a cheerful insincerity which appealed to a wide and uncritical audience, his repertoire and performances were, indeed, "severe" and quite a contrast to those organists of whom a contemporary critic wrote,". . . they prostitute our organs to the barcarolle, contredanse, galop, valse, and polka."[63] And it was his severe taste which kept his name from being added to the lists Cavaillé-Coll submitted to churches of organists he recommended to inaugurate their new organs.[64]

Certain adjectives have appeared in the preceding accounts of Franck's public performances which describe his organ playing: "skillful," "masterful," "knowledgeable," "energetic," "severe," "subtle," "magisterial." Indeed these adjectives are synonymous with

---

[63] *Revue et Gazette musicale de Paris* (13 July 1845) 232. And Adolph Hesse, on a trip in 1844, observed that organ playing in France was ". . . generally irreverent, although once in a while a significant talent came to my attention within this irreverence. Not rarely does one hear a gay pastorale during a church service, which turns into a thunderstorm before closing with a sort of operatic grand finale in free style. Given that this is untenable from the German/religious point of view, it must be admitted that such things are often done quite talentedly. A requiem mass for Lafitte in St. Roch Church gave me the opportunity to hear one M. Lefébure-Wély play in a solemn, appropriate manner, whereas he worked up a tremendously gay mood during the mass on Sunday. In response to my astonishment over this I was told that clergy as well as the congregation expect light-hearted music." (Adolph Friedrich Hesse, "Einiges über Orgeln, deren Einrichtung und Behandlung in Österreich, Italien, Frankreich und England," *Neuen Zeitschrift für Musik,* 1853, 53)

[64] One such list, sent to the church of La Madeleine in Tarare suggested Parisian organists Cavallo, Simon, Durand and Saint-Saëns. And thirteen-year-old "Charles Marie Widor" of Lyon who would gladly play the dedication for a modest fee." (Letter of 16 March 1857. Quoted by Fenner Douglass in *Cavaillé-Coll and the Musicians,* 2 vols.. [Raleigh: Sunbury, 1980] Vol. I, 363)

those that describe Franck the pianist.[65] While the pianist's "warmth," "feeling," and "expressiveness" would hardly retain the same connotation when transferred to the organ, the similarity of the other adjectives is immediately apparent.

Maurice Emmanuel even felt that Franck was ". . . more pianist than organist . . ."[66] and expands on this statement citing that "Franck was little preoccupied with absolute legato."[67] But here he seems to be referring more to Franck's organ works than to his actual playing, for he cites certain passages in the organ music such as the large, awkward stretches[68] (as in the *Prière* and *First Choral*) and his frequent use of repeated chords (*Pastorale, Fantaisie en la*, and *Pièce héroïque*), attributing them to Franck's inability to arpeggiate on the organ.

With the exception of Vincent d'Indy, who was in Franck's organ class from 1873 to 1875, all the students who wrote testimonies of Franck's playing had heard him improvise or demonstrate certain points at lessons. The only primary sources which discuss his playing (and those only in general terms) were the accounts in contemporary musical journals.

---

[65] In spite of the differences between the organ and the piano we note the similarities of Franck's interpretive powers. I quote nine descriptive comments of Franck as a pianist ranging throughout his career.

His piano teachers at the Liège Conservatoire mentioned the eleven-year-old boy's ". . . tendency towards warmth of feeling which sometimes becomes mere daubing. . . ." (Vallas, *Franck*, 15) ". . . ease, self-possession, intelligence, passionate energy, expressiveness and musical feeling." (*Revue et Gazette musicale de Paris*, 4 June 1837, 194) ". . . the brilliance, vigor, and precision of his playing." (*Revue et Gazette musicale de Paris*, 31 March 1839) ". . . ease and suppleness of his technique." (*Ibid.*, 17 Jan. 1839, 27) "M. C.-A. Franck sweeps all difficulties out of his path as he proceeds. His fingers are extraordinarily lively; he is by turns mellow and energetic, elegant and warm-hearted, brilliant yet constructive in his style of playing. . . . he exhibited a sense of phrasing which is rare." (*Ibid.*, 1 March 1840, 144) ". . . played with a modesty only equaled by his persuasive expressiveness." (*Ibid.*, 2 May 1841, 249) ". . . his piano playing is fluent, crisp and sparkling." (*Ibid.*, 5 Feb. 1843, 15) ". . . an elegant and expressive pianist." (*Ibid.*, 11 Jan. 1880, 15) "His playing was profound, both clear and pathetic, exempt from affectation and rhetoric." (Maurice Emmanuel, *César Franck*, [Paris: Laurens, 1930] 101)

[66] Emmanuel, *Ibid*. And he continues ". . . yet, more musician than technician."

[67] *Ibid.*

[68] His unusually large hands enabled him to span a twelfth easily. (Norbert Dufourcq, *La musique d'orgue français de Jehan Titelouse à Jehan Alain* [Paris: Floury, 1949] 151)

While he performed little in public[69] in the last decade of his life, Franck did play at private gatherings of friends and students.[70] He had by this time completely devoted himself to composition.

Those who heard him say that his virtuosity was limited. But this was of little importance to him as he often said when playing from his own music, "I play it badly, but you understand me all the same."[71]

The similarities between Franck's organ and piano playing identify him with a common French style and technique which, according to Marguerite Long, is ". . . characterized by such attributes as gracefulness, clarity, suppleness, elegance and moderation."[72]

---

[69] Paderewski (Ignace Paderewski and Mary Lawton, *The Paderewski Memoirs* [New York: Scribner, 1938] 141) wrote that Franck ". . . was never to be seen in concerts [in the 1880's]. He was living like a monk, seeing only his pupils, and it is generally believed that he was actually afraid of new acquaintances. He retired absolutely from life."

[70] It was at these gatherings that Emmanuel (*Franck*, 110–11) heard Franck play the Adagio from Beethoven's *Sonata*, Op. 10, No. 3, Chopin's *Préludes* (Nos. 4, 9, 10, 13, 15, 17, 21 and 25) and *Études* (Nos. 9 and 11).

[71] Cellier et Bachelin, *L'Orgue*, 242.

[72] Marguerite Long, *Le Piano* (Paris: Salabert, 1959) ii.

CHAPTER THREE

CÉSAR FRANCK – PROFESSOR OF ORGAN

⋖꒰ꎇ꒱⋗

The circumstances which led to the appointment in 1872 of César Franck as professor of organ at the Paris Conservatoire are uncertain. Théodore Dubois, director of the Paris Conservatoire from 1896 to 1905, had been maître de chapelle at Sainte-Clotilde from 1859 to 1861 and from 1866 to 1868. With Franck and Saint Saëns he had been a founder of the Société Nationale in 1871. In a speech at the unveiling of the Franck monument in the square in front of Sainte-Clotilde he declared:

> When the professorship of organ fell vacant . . . I at once sought out my principal, Ambroise Thomas, and said to him, "There is at the moment one man only who is fit for the post, and that is César Franck." He replied with only these words: "That is correct," and had him appointed.[1]

Camille Saint-Saëns claimed for himself the responsibility for Franck's appointment:

> Jules Simon, then Minister of Education, had consulted me on the choice of a professor of organ at the Conservatoire and I strongly recommended

---

[1] Théodore Dubois, "Discours," *Souvenir du 22 octôbre 1904*, 20. Charles Marie Widor ("La classe d'orgue du Conservatoire," *Le Ménestrel*, 3 June 1921, 237), Franck's successor as professor of organ at the Paris Conservatoire, verifies Dubois's account and describes the procedure for the appointment:
"Dubois recommended Franck to Thomas. As the nomination of professors then did not depend on a *conseil superieur*, the director proposed three candidates for the signature of the Minister [of Fine Arts] who traditionally chose the first on the list."

him to choose César Franck so that the latter, with the help of the salary granted by the state, might not find himself compelled to waste in giving piano lessons the time he could more profitably devote to composition.[2]

Saint-Saëns was convinced of his benevolence toward Franck for on two other occasions he repeated this anecdote: in a letter (23 November 1915) to Léon Vallas[3] and in a letter (1917) to the eighteen-year-old Francis Poulenc[4] who had asked for his thoughts on César Franck.

Cavaillé-Coll is also credited with having been instrumental in engineering Franck's appointment. His biographers relate that after the death of Lefébure-Wély (on New Year's Eve, 1869) both Franck and Widor presented themselves for the very desirable post at Saint-Sulpice.

> A close friend of Franck for twenty years, a profound admirer and upholder of his genius, then so unrecognized, Cavaillé-Coll opted, however, for Widor. . . . Gounod, an arbitrator chosen by the chapter of Saint-Sulpice, settled the question. Widor prevailed. At first, Franck was deeply hurt, but this great man would not lower himself to bear a grudge; he forgot his rivalry and remained the friend of Cavaillé-Coll, whose sincerity had touched him a little unkindly. What Cavaillé-Coll wished for Franck was a chair of composition at the Conservatoire. He asked for it discreetly and Franck was nominated . . . head of the organ class, succeeding Benoist.[5]

Vincent d'Indy concludes: ". . . he was appointed, nobody knows how—and he himself, a stranger to all intrigue, understood it less than rest . . . the mystery has never been elucidated."[6]

On 1 February 1872, when he succeeded his former teacher François Benoist, Franck's annual salary as professor of organ was 1,500 francs. Over the years it rose to 2,400 francs per year.[7]

Three classes a week on Tuesday, Thursday, and Saturday mornings from eight to ten o'clock were held in the same hall as Benoist's had

[2] Camille Saint-Saëns, *Les idées de Monsieur Vincent d'Indy* (Paris: Lafitte, 1918). Translated by Fred Rothwell and included in *Outspoken Essays on Music*, originally published in 1922 (New York: Books for Libraries Press, 1969) 46.

[3] Vallas, *Franck*, 138.

[4] Francis Poulenc, *Emmanuel Chabrier* (Paris: La Palatine, 1961) 112–13.

[5] Cécile et Emmanuel Cavaillé-Coll, *Aristide Cavaillé-Coll* (Paris: Fischbacher, 1929) 125–26.

[6] d'Indy, *Franck*, 46.

[7] Gallois, *Franck*, 97.

been. A different organ, if not much better, at least newer, had been installed in 1871. When the hall was in use for examinations, Franck would change the hour or adjourn to a piano classroom and concentrate on plainsong.[8]

The curriculum for Franck's organ class was the same as it had been when he was a student thirty years before. Widor's charge that ". . . he was content to teach a free improvisation class based on the immutable *andante*"[9] is less severe when we understand that Franck had to submit to the strict rules for the departmental examinations. However, ". . . far from being disheartened, his imagination was excited and stimulated to overcome the difficulties by attention to details."[10]

With Franck the study of fugue was "essentially classical, but expanded."[11]

> In fugue he was particularly interested in the construction of the episodes, combining an ingenious tonal plan with the elegant writing of a counterpoint with imitations in closer and closer stretto.
>
> Every now and then he would sit down at the keyboard and give us an example. And what an example! While we had difficulty working out one correct counter-subject, he, in the same time, had found five or six: "See, you can do this . . . or else this . . . or again. . . ." Then, in the most natural tone: "Come, now choose one and make me a good fugue!"[12]

In the free improvisation Franck was interested in everything that touched upon musical expression; melodic invention, harmonic discoveries, subtle modulations, and formal elegance.[13]

> For the free subject he found a way of stretching the strict form, either by subtly introducing a new element at the moment of transition to the

[8] Vierne, *Mes Souvenirs*, 22.

[9] Widor, "La classe d'orgue," 237.

[10] Vierne, *Mes Souvenirs*, 24.

[11] Tournemire, *Franck*, 70.

[12] Vierne, *Mes Souvenirs*, 24. Tournemire (*Franck*, 71) mirrors Vierne's description of the organ class:
"The art of improvisation was carried to an extraordinary degree of intensity. The method of teaching was by example. As soon as he suggested a fugue subject our master immediately sat at the console and almost spontaneously found several counter-subjects. We had only to choose; . . . but, this luxury of 'resources' was, for us, a source of great difficulties. We put ourselves, in turn, at the bewitched claviers . . . and, alas! we so often got lost! Impossible to extricate ourselves. And every time Franck said, impatiently, 'But, I'm showing you!' This was said in a deep paternal voice."

[13] Vierne, *Mes Souvenirs*, 32.

dominant, an element which could serve later in the development, or by the intensive cultivation in the development of a new theme suggested by a fragment of the given theme. Inversion was cultivated vigorously as was the change of rhythm; or an ostinato pattern used with a definite intention and taken from a fragment of the theme; or a variety and subtlety of harmonization. All were artifices which the maître could handle with disconcerting ease.[14]

Tournemire elaborates upon this aspect of the improvisation class;

> We based our improvisations on the sonata-allegro which allowed us to create a second theme and subsequently, to combine it with the mother theme according to necessity. How "amusing" the invariable observation, however, while we were painstakingly finishing the first part, not without trouble.
>
> "Something else!" These two words of the maître pulled us out of a relative torpor.
>
> Then—and this was inevitable—our incompetence made us noisily kick the swell pedal.
>
> And we set sail and moved ahead according to our ability. When there was danger we were always saved.
>
> The return to the theme was much sought for. How we loved to remember "Papa's" advice: subtlety, the unexpected. When we succeeded, a sound: "I like it," elated us.
>
> This was our teacher: an educator full of fire with a marvelous heart.[15]

Because five of the six hours a week of the organ class were devoted to improvisation, little time was spent on performance.[16] Although Franck regarded his duties as professor of organ seriously (he told Louis de Serres, in 1885, "When you join my class, young man, your job is to play the organ!" And he repeated slowly, "to play the organ"),[17] he followed no prescribed course of instruction. Guillaume Lekeu noted the absence of textbooks in Franck's class[18] —he was even unfamiliar with Bazin's treatise on harmony—the Conservatoire's standard text.

Three organ methods were in circulation and readily accessible dur-

---

[14] *Ibid.*, 24.

[15] Tournemire, *Franck*, 71.

[16] Vierne, *Mes Souvenirs*, 23.

[17] Louis de Serres, "Quelques souvenirs sur le père Franck, mon maître," *l'Art musical* (Paris: 1936). Quoted in Vallas, *Franck*, 254.

[18] Guillaume Lekeu, "Lettres inédites," *Courrier musical* (Jan.–Dec. 1906). Quoted in Davies, *Franck and His Circle*, 245.

ing Franck's tenure at the Conservatoire: Rinck's classic method[19] had been brought out by Richault in a French edition in 1833 under the title *École d'orgue pratique;* Lemmens' *École d'orgue* appeared in 1862 (parts of which had been available since 1850);[20] and Lemmens' student, Clément Loret, organ teacher at École Niedermeyer, had published his own method in 1858.[21]

Vierne mentions that when he was a student at the Institution Nationale des Jeunes Aveugles, his teacher, Louis Lebel, had his students study only the "pedal school" of the Lemmens method—it being taken for granted that the students knew the part concerning the manuals.[22] Then, when a student entered Franck's class at the Conservatoire, it was assumed that he "possessed an instrumental technique sufficient for the interpretation of all Bach . . . ."[23]

Matters of organ construction and registration were never touched upon. "I confess that, except for guessing by the sound, I did not really know the harmonic difference between a Plein jeu and a Cornet, and much less between a Nasard and a Quinte."[24]

The students had limited repertoires and scarcely prepared more than the pieces intended for the examinations in January and June.[25] In these pieces Franck, never meticulous about technical details, would give almost too much help with registration or expressive pedaling.[26]

> There was no need to worry about manipulation; Franck drew the stops, worked the combination pedals, managed the swell pedal. Everything was simplified, reduced merely to the playing on the keyboards and the observance of style.[27]

[19] C. H. Rinck, *Practische Orgelschule*, Op. 56 (Berlin: Simrock, c. 1794).

[20] Jacques Lemmens, *Journal d'orgue* (Brussels, 1850).

[21] Clément Loret, *Cours d'orgue et exercise journalier* (Paris: La Maîtrise, 1858–1859).

[22] Vierne, *Mes Souvenirs*, 15.

[23] *Ibid.*, 23.

[24] *Ibid.*, 40.

[25] *Ibid.*, 23.

[26] Vallas, *Franck*, 254.

[27] Vierne, *Mes Souvenirs*, 23. John Hinton (*Franck*, 6) mentions that when he studied privately with Franck in 1867 his copy of the *Well-Tempered Clavier* (purist prejudices did not preclude its study) was returned by Franck ". . . with the first twelve numbers (both Preludes and Fugues) fingered in places of difficulty and marked with pedaling for optional use on the organ."

The organ repertoire studied in Franck's class included, among other things, the major organ works of Bach. (A partial list can be found in Appendix B.) Few of his own works were played at the *concours* but Franck did not hesitate to give advice on their performance to pupils who occasionally brought them to class.[28]

Three of Franck's frequently repeated maxims are worth quoting:

> Don't try to do a great deal, but rather seek to do *well* no matter if only a little can be produced.

> Bring me the results of many trials which you can honestly say represent the very best you can do.

> Don't think that you will learn from my corrections of faults *of which you are aware* unless you have strained every effort yourself to amend them.[29]

Franck was a wonderfully affable man: warm, generous, good. His "observations, said in a few words, generally soft and penetrating, impressive and just, enlightened the soul and warmed the heart."[30] Vierne writes:

> Of Franck I had made almost a religion, combining passionate admiration, filial affection and profound respect. I experienced with intense joy, with which, however, there was also mingled a certain mysterious awe, the almost magnetic fascination which emanated from that man at the same time, so simple, so natural, so truly good.[31]

Franck's earlier impression on the fifteen-year-old Vierne was no different: "The low-pitched, slow and gentle voice of César Franck gave me a sensation of physical pleasure from which a certain mysterious awe was not excluded.[32]

Franck's rich, deep voice, his beatific, unlined countenance and personal magnetism drew the young disciples to him. He smothered

---

[28] Vierne, *Mes Souvenirs*, 23.

[29] Hinton, *Franck*, 6.

[30] Tournemire, *Franck*, 70.

[31] Vierne, *Mes Souvenirs,* 18.

[32] *Ibid.*, 14.

them with kindness and fatherly affection. But he was a conscientious teacher, and the peaceful atmosphere of the class was not infrequently interrupted by explosions of wrath " . . . when awkward finger went astray . . . in some ugly harmonic progression."[33] Hinton recalled that "wrong accidentals in playing particularly annoyed him . . . he would shout and even rave like a madman if the offense were repeated."[34]

Left with such vivid memories of their Pater Seraphicus, his students— both Tournemire and Vierne were almost twenty when Franck died—keenly felt and long remembered his influence. It is doubtful that either man forgot a moment spent in the presence of César Franck.

It was as the Conservatoire's Professor of Organ that Franck was awarded the Legion of Honor.

> It was, I think, in 1886 that the Minister of Fine Arts granted Franck the Legion of Honor, and it was upon this occasion—the only official recognition which Franck ever received—that I heard him pronounce the only repining word that perhaps ever passed his lips. When I was congratulating him upon this honor, he replied rather sadly: "Yes, my friend, they honor me as a Professor!" No doubt the thought then uppermost in his mind was this, that in high places he was still ignored as a composer.[35]

At the end of the academic year the students competed for the first prize. There were never more than four students competing in any given year. In Franck's first nine years as professor of organ only three students won first prize: Paul Wachs (1872), who had been in Benoist's class, Samuel Rousseau (1877) and Henri Dallier (1878). Vincent d'Indy won only first accessit in 1875 and never competed again.

The jury comprised nine members—eight jurors and the director of the Conservatoire, Ambroise Thomas—throughout Franck's tenure. In July 1873, the jury for the "Concours d'orgue, contrepoint et fugue" comprised Ambroise Thomas, François Benoist, Georges Bizet, Jules Cohen, Duprato, Eugène Gatier, Henri Fissot, Jules Massenet, and Camille Saint-Saëns.

---

[33] d'Indy, *Franck*, 67.

[34] HInton, *Franck*, 6.

[35] Ropartz, "Franck," 79. When the Société Internationale des Organistes et Maîtres-de-Chapelle was founded by J. Vasseur in 1881 César Franck served on the jury for the concours with Dubois, Gigout, Lefèvre, Loret and Steenmann. (Henri Letocart, "Quelques souvenirs II," *L'Orgue*, No. 37 [March 1939] 5).

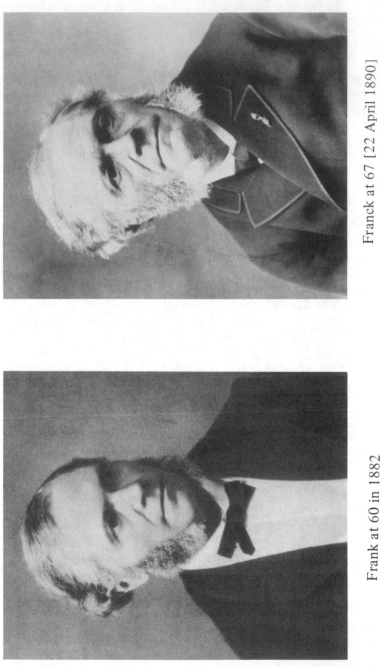

Franck at 67 [22 April 1890]

Frank at 60 in 1882

An account of César Franck, organ teacher, would hardly be complete without a list of his students. Below is as complete a list as is possible to compile at this time. All of the students in the organ class who were awarded prizes are identified by numbers within parenthesis. Roman numerals (I, II) indicate First and Second Prize. Arabic numerals (1, 2) indicate First and Second Accessits. Names marked with an asterisk studied composition privately with Franck. Hinton and Woodman studied organ privately.

Georges Aubry (2: 1888)
Alfred Bachelet
Camille Benoît
Louis Benoît Bazile,
    dit (2: 1872)
Georges Paul Bondon
    (I: 1889)
Mélanie Bonis
Josephine Boulay
    (I: 1888)
Jules Bouval
Pierre de Bréville
Burgat
Henri Busser
Albert Cahen*
Alexis de Castillon
Auguste Chapuis (I: 1881)
Ernest Chausson*
Charles Collin
Arthur Coquard*
Henri Dallier (I: 1878)
Georges-Philippe Deslandres
Edmond-Marie Diet
Henri Duparc*
A. Dutacq
Jules Écorcheville
Henry Expert*
Dynam-Victor Fumet
César Galleotti (I: 1887)
Louis Ganne (1: 1882)
Marie-Louise Gentry
    (2: 1876)
Anatole-Léon Grand-Jany
    (I: 1883)

Georges Guiraud
John Hinton*
Augusta Holmès*
Joseph-Paul Humblot
    (II: 1873)
Vincent d'Indy (2: 1874)
Paul-Joseph Jeannin
    (1: 1882)
Jean-Jacques Jemain
    (1: 1887)
Henri Kaiser (1: 1884)
Henri Kunkelmann
Louis Landry (1: 1884)
Fernand de La Tombelle
Fernand Leborne
Guillaume Lekeu*
Henri Letocart (2: 1887)
Henri Libert
Albert Mahaut (I: 1889)
Adolphe Marty (I: 1886)
Georges-Eugène Marty
Carlos Mesquita (2: 1884)
Marie-Anna Papot (II: 1879)
Gabriel Pierné (I: 1882)
Henri Pinot
Marie Prestat (I: 1890)
Henri Quittard
Camille Rage
Albert Renaud
Marie-Léonie Renaud
    (I: 1876)
J. Guy Ropartz
Paul Rougnon

Samuel Rousseau
 (I: 1877)
Achille Runner
Gabriel Saint-Réné-
 Taillandier
Alice Sauvrezis
Schneider
Louis de Serres
Pierre Sourilas (1: 1880)
Ternisien
Jean Tolbecque (1: 1873)

Charles Tournemire
 (1: 1890)
Gaston de Vallin
Georges Verschneider
 (1: 1875)
Paul Vidal
Louis Vierne
Paul Wachs (I: 1872)
Paul de Wailly*
R. Huntington Woodman*

CHAPTER FOUR

THE CAVAILLÉ-COLL ORGAN

〜♋〜

TONAL CHARACTERISTICS

In the middle of the nineteenth century, the three-hundred-year-old tradition of the polyphonic organ in France yielded to the demands of romantic composers as many classic instruments underwent renovation and rebuilding.

[Cavaillé-Coll] modified the balance of sonorities in his instrument. He was not content to endow it with a swell box (a chamber with walls formed by shutters movable at the will of the performer) enclosing all of the pipework of one manual—the third, or Récit—which, from then on, grew unexpectedly; he transformed the composition of the very organ which had been standardized by the organ builders of the time of Louis XIII. He abandoned the essential characteristic of the organ of Robert Clicquot—the *Plein jeu*. Compound and simple mixtures, Fournitures and Cymbales, Nasards, Larigots and Tierce séparée—all of those stops which represented the family of harmonics intended to enrich the fundamental pitch—disappeared. If he still maintained a Plein jeu or a Cornet on one of the divisions of the instrument, it was less to preserve the sonorities of the classic organ than it was to balance the reeds and add brilliance to their upper register. From then on the polyphonic organ disappeared. It was succeeded by a symphonic organ that was infinitely less clear, more compact, without doubt of greater brilliance but also of lesser stature. Numerous foundation stops borrowed from foreign organs replaced the abandoned registers. Cavaillé-Coll enriched each manual with stops called *harmoniques* or *octaviants* which were to be used as solo stops. The Flûte harmonique, the most prevalent type, added a freshness of color to a fullness of sound. Finally, the differently timbred old reeds were replaced by sonorous batteries (16', 8', 4') which, when combined, in-

47

creased the power of the *tutti*. To the old reeds, such as the Cromorne, the Voix humaine or the Trompette, were added some free-reed stops intended to imitate orchestral instruments: the Clarinet and English Horn. Not the least of those innovations credited to Cavaillé-Coll was an enrichment of the pedal division with several 16' foundation stops and an enlargement of its composition. From then on, this became fundamental just as it had been with builders in Germany for two centuries.

Thus, the symphonic organ was created. After 1840, the extreme diversity (32' to 1') of foundation stops, mutations and reeds, was succeeded by a profusion of stops of the same family—foundation and reeds—which directed everything toward the single 8' pitch. This uniform instrument which followed a horizontal plan, succeeded the organ arranged in pitch according to the gradation of harmonics.[1]

MECHANICAL CHARACTERISTICS

In the churches of France the organ stands in a gallery at the west end of the building.[2] The console of Cavaillé-Coll's organs was below the level of the pipes, generally in front of and detached from the case and in a reversed position so that the player sat with his back to the organ and looked over the console and down into the church. By the middle of the nineteenth century this console and its appointments attained a uniformity of design hitherto unknown in the organ world. An organist "did not need five minutes to feel as much at home on one organ as another " built by Cavaillé-Coll.[3]

The order of manuals, from lowest to highest, was invariably (I) Grand-Orgue, (II) Positif and (III) Récit. On four-manual consoles the Bombarde was located between the Grand-Orgue and the Positif; the fifth manual, the Grand-Choeur, was positioned below the Grand-Orgue.

As much as Cavaillé-Coll changed the sound of the traditional organ, so too he improved the mechanical action of the instrument:

> The large instrument built by Cavaillé-Coll for the Abbey of Saint-Denis (1841) marked a turning point in the history of the organ. This builder's

---

[1] Dufourcq, *La musique d'orgue française*, 137–38. Translated by Raymond Mabry in *Music* VIII/6 (June 1974) 32–33. [Emended by the author.]

[2] Unlike most continental churches, Sainte-Clotilde is built on a north-south axis rather than east and west. Instead of the organ gallery in its traditional west-end position, Sainte-Clotilde's is located at the north end.

[3] Albert Schweitzer, *Deutsche und französische Orgelbaukunst und Orgelkunst* (Leipzig: Breitkopf & Härtel, 1906) 5.

new concept was the source of all music composed from the first years of the Second Empire (1852–1870) until the war of 1914–1918. First, he perfected the wind supply and the mechanism, both of which left something to to be desired. He gave his organ new lungs in the form of reservoirs and boxes intended to equalize the bellows. He increased the wind pressure in order to augment the power of the full organ, and invented bellows of diverse pressures. Moreover, he gave his organ some motory nerves, under the form of a pneumatic machine which bears the name of its inventor—Barker —and which permits, if not always a lighter touch, at least the coupling of several manuals without making the touch heavier. Some iron pedals or *tirasses*, placed at the level of the feet permitted one to introduce or to cancel certain stops by a simple pressure. Finally, although the manual keyboards did not undergo any transformation, they were constructed with greater care and their range extended to fifty-six notes. The impracticable row of pegs, which the organist had to play with his feet, was replaced by the long keys of the German pedal keyboard, and it is this which—facilitating pedal virtuosity and introducing in France the use of the heel in pedal playing—gives to the bass an importance previously unknown.[4]

THE PÉDALES DE COMBINAISON

Across the front of the console, immediately above the pedalboard, were iron ratchet pedals which controlled certain mechanical contrivances designed to assist the organist in manipulating the stops and couplers. These pedals were held depressed by being moved to the left or right under a notch. The subtle use of these pédales de combinaison gave the French symphonic organ composers command of their tonal resources and enabled them to make rapid crescendi from the soft voices of the enclosed Récit to the full power of the organ with just a few movements. These pédales de combinaison were arranged in groups and the order within each group was determined by the order of the manuals—from the lowest to the highest.

Tirasses: pedal couplers which coupled each manual to the pedalboard. When engaged, the tirasse mechanically and visibly pulled down the manual key which corresponded to the pedal note.

Octaves graves: sub-octave couplers, affecting the same manual, which depress the note an octave below the note played.

Anches: this term, although strictly translating as "reeds," included those ranks above four-foot pitch as well as mixtures and reeds. The Hautbois and Voix humaïne were always excluded from this category.

---

[4] Dufourcq, *La musique d'orgue française*, 137. [Emended by the author.]

The drawknobs for this group of stops were lettered in red and a ventil pedal controlled the wind supply to the pipes.[5] Any combination of these anches could be prepared in advance and, even though the stop knob was drawn, the pipes would not speak until the corresponding pédale de combinaison was depressed.

Accouplements: couplers permitting one manual to be played on another. Accomplished by direct mechanical linkage, this coupling device visibly operates the keys of the manuals involved. If the Récit were coupled to the Positif and the organist played on the latter manual, the identical keys of the Récit would go down. If the Positif were then coupled to the Grand-Orgue and the organist played on that manual, both the keys of the Positif and those of the Récit (if coupled to the Positif) would go down. If the Tirasse Grand-Orgue or pedal coupler, described above, were depressed and a pedal note played, the corresponding note on all three keyboards would also go down.

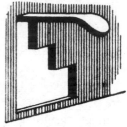

Expression de Récit: the pedal at the far right controlling the vertical shutters of the chamber in which the pipes of the Récit were enclosed. These shutters were kept tightly closed by a spring.[6] When the box was opened, the organist's foot had to remain on the pedal unless it were hitched into one of the two notches at the side which held the shutter either half-open or fully open.

Pédale d'expression de Récit

In spite of the high degree of standardization, Cavaillé-Coll did indulge in some pecularities from organ to organ. A perusal of the specifications in Appendix C will make this obvious. For instance, the very large organs (Saint-Étienne-du-Mont, Saint-Sulpice and Notre-Dame-de-Paris) had no Récit au Positif coupler and the only manual which coupled to the Pédale was the Grand-Orgue (and Grand-Choeur, when present). Sainte-Clotilde had Octaves graves for each division, but other organs had this device only for the Récit or the Grand-Orgue. These inconsistencies necessitated some modification of the formula for the operation of the pédales de combinaison.

From about 1850 until the present, French organ composers have based their compositions on the basic tonal structure that follows. The

[5] Wallace Goodrich, *The Organ in France* (Boston: Boston Music Company, 1917) 38.

[6] C. A. Edwards, *Organs and Organ Building* (London: "The Bazaar" Office, 1881) 122.

Fonds (foundation stops which give the tone at the pitch played—8', at the octave below—16', or at the octave above—4') were drawn on each manual and Pédale. The stops of the Grand-Orgue did not sound because the Grand-Orgue sur machine or Grand-Orgue Introduction had to be activated which connected that manual with the Barker lever machine.[7]   The Tirasse Grand-Orgue was depressed so that whatever stops played on the Grand-Orgue would also play in the Pédale. Next, the anches were drawn on each division but, because their corresponding ventil pedals were not depressed, they did not sound. When playing on the Grand-Orgue, the Récit was coupled in first and was then followed by the Positif. The stops of the Grand-Orgue were brought in when the Grand-Orgue Introduction was depressed.

If other manual couplers were present (i.e., Récit au Positif) or if the Récit did not couple to the Grand-Orgue (as at Sainte-Clotilde), the following procedure (always followed by César Franck) was adopted: the same registration as above was prepared and the Récit au Positif and Positif au Grand-Orgue couplers were activated. The organist began the crescendo playing on the Récit. When more tone was desired he dropped down to the Positif manual and, if using the Pédale division, added the Tirasse Positif. He then moved down to the Grand-Orgue manual and depressed the Tirasse Grand-Orgue. With the Fonds of all the manuals now sounding, the swell box could be closed—the Positif and Grand-Orgue stops partially masking the disappearance of those of the Récit. Now the Anches Récit was depressed. The gradual opening of the swell box increased the sound in proportion to how many stops among the anches were drawn (the selection of registers depended upon the desired intensity of the height of the crescendo). When the Récit was fully open, the Positif anches were added followed by those of the Grand-Orgue. All divisions being coupled to the Pédale, whatever affected the manuals also affected the Pédale. The final addition was the Anches Pédale. A decrescendo was brought about by reversing this process.

Because all nuances were controlled by the feet, the hands need never leave the keys to touch a stop or a mechanical accessory during the course of an entire movement.

[7] Patented in France by its inventor, the Englishman Charles Spackman Barker (1806–1879), the Barker machine is a pneumatic lever in the form of a small bellows positioned between the key and the pull-down mechanism below the pallet of the windchest. It was adopted by Cavaillé-Coll to lighten the touch and reduce the key-dip of the Grand-Orgue, the keyboard to which all the other manuals of the organ were coupled.

Church of Sainte-Clotilde

CHAPTER FIVE

THE ORGAN OF SAINTE-CLOTILDE

An authentic interpretation of the organ music of César Franck is dependent upon an understanding of the mechanical and tonal characteristics of the French organs of the second half of the nineteenth century, particularly those instruments built by Aristide Cavaillé-Coll, and specifically the 3-manual, 46-stop organ in the Basilica of Sainte-Clotilde over which, as has been stated, Franck presided as titulaire from 1859 until his death in 1890. Although Franck had played many of the important organs of the French capital, the fact that his music was composed with the organ of Sainte-Clotilde in mind is obvious from the printed indications and testimony from his contemporaries: "All of his organ music was written for this instrument. This explains the plans and the particular registrations."[1]

---

[1] Louis Vierne, *Journal* (Paris: Les Amis de l'Orgue, 1970) 155. And Joseph Bonnet ("Preface," *César Franck's Three Chorals*, dated New York, July–Sept. 1942, but published [New York: Fischer, 1948] 2), noting the similarities between Franck's music and his organ at Sainte-Clotilde, writes:

> "It is obvious that, in writing his organ works, César Franck was much impressed by this special organ, and planned his registration according to the resources of the Sainte-Clotilde instrument."

These statements may, indeed, be true, but there are several inconsistencies between Franck's organ music and the organ of Sainte-Clotilde. The *Six Pièces* were not published until 1868 (Norbert Dufourcq, *César Franck et la genèse des premières oeuvres d'orgue* [Paris: Les Amis de l'Orgue, 1973] 10)—by Maeyens-Couvreur—and, as we have seen, Franck was familiar with a number of organs.

In his Pédale registration Franck variously calls for "Fonds," "Flûte," and "Bourdon." The first two terms are synonymous with the 16' Contrebasse and 8' Flûte (or Basse) which appear on the Sainte-Clotilde specification, but "Bour-

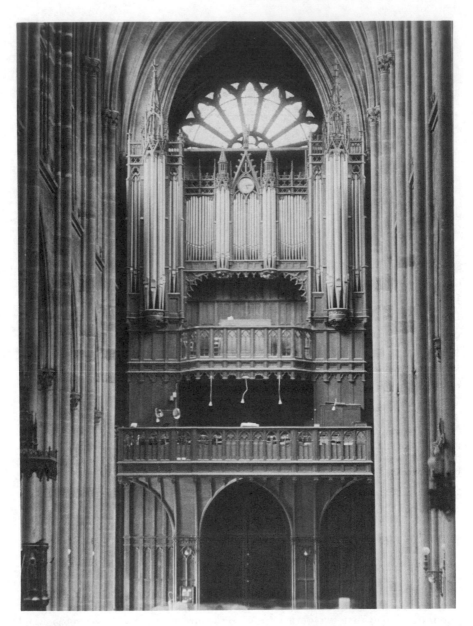

Sainte-Clotilde, North Wall

Carsten Lund

Among the organs of Paris in the 1860's that of Sainte-Clotilde was neither modest nor unique. It was small in comparison with the two hallmark Cavaillé-Colls of the French capital: Saint-Sulpice (5 manuals, 100 stops) and Notre-Dame-de-Paris (5 manuals, 86 stops) whose organists, Charles Marie Widor (1844–1937) and Louis Vierne (1870–1937), share with Franck the fame of the romantic French organ school. There were other large organs (Saint-Denis, 5 manuals, 70 stops; Saint-Eustache, 4 manuals, 67 stops; and later, the Trocadéro, 4 manuals, 66 stops), but these were the exceptions. Most three-manual instruments were relatively the same size as that of Sainte-Clotilde.

THE CONSOLE

The Cavaillé-Coll organ console of Sainte-Clotilde stood on a platform a few feet in front of the case. It was reversed and low enough so that the organist could see over it, down the nave, and follow the movements of the priest on the altar. Franck's original console was replaced in 1933. It is now in Mechelen, Belgium in the music room of the eminent organist and composer, Flor Peeters.[2]

The console has three manuals of 54 keys and a pedalboard of 27 notes. The straight stop knobs (with round shanks) are arranged in four horizontal rows on terraced jambs on either side of the keyboards.

don" was a stopped flue-pipe rank and unavailable on the organ of Saint-Clotilde.

In the second *Andante* of the *Grande Pièce symphonique* Franck calls for the Récit coupled to the Positif with the Voix céleste drawn on each manual. There was no organ at that time on which this 22-bar work could be authentically performed. Cavaillé-Coll had experimented with the location of the Voix céleste (on the organ of La Madeleine it was on the Positif and on the organ of Saint-Vincent-de-Paul it was on the Grand-Orgue) before deciding on what was to be its traditional place—the Récit. But he only included one Voix céleste on each organ. And later, if he added a second undulating stop, it was always called by another name—Unda maris—as at Saint-Sulpice, where it was included on the Positif. The manuscript of the *Grande Pièce symphonique* bears the date September 16, 1863. We do not know if Franck played it at the inauguration of the Saint-Sulpice organ in 1862. Surely, the effect of two undulating stops coupled together would have appealed to the composer of a symphonic piece for a symphonic organ who once commented with delight that his new organ was an orchestra!

In the initial registration of the *Final*, Franck calls for "Fonds et Anches de 4, 8, et 16 pieds" on the Récit—yet he had no stops of 16' pitch on that division.

The Pédale of the Sainte-Clotilde organ extended only to 'D, but in the *Fantaisie en la*, Franck has written an 'F (providing an alternate reading at the octave below.) In the *Second Choral*, Franck has written ' ' 'F♯ (m. 233) yet the manuals on his instrument extended only to ' ' 'F.

[2] Flor Peeters, Letter to the author (Mechelen, 27 April 1981).

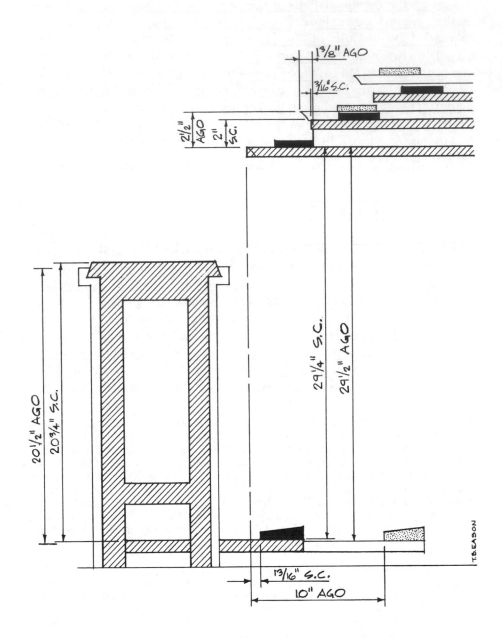

1³/₈" AGO

³/₁₆" S.C.

2¹/₂" AGO

2" S.C.

20¹/₂" AGO

20³/₄" S.C.

29¹/₄" S.C.

29¹/₂" AGO

13/16" S.C.

10" AGO

T.B.EASON

Sainte-Clotilde Console Measurements
Compared with the American Guild of Organists Standard of 1961
Sainte-Clotilde (S. C.) ▨ ■   AGO Standard (AGO) ▭ ▨

The ivory key coverings are square at the front and overhang the vertical front—like piano keys. The pedalboard is flat and parallel.

The dimensions of César Franck's console become relevant when we compare them with a modern console. We have chosen for comparison the console dimensions approved in 1961 by the American Guild of Organists.[3] The diagram opposite illustrates their similarities and differences.

Because all registrational changes are affected by the feet, thumb pistons between the manuals are nonexistent on nineteenth century French organs; hence, the keyboards are closer together. The distance between the surface of the natural keys of one manual and that of the one above or below is two inches. Franck's keyboards are half an inch closer than those of American organs.

On Franck's console the front edges of the keys of one manual extend only 3/16ths of an inch over those of the manual below. On American organs the manual overhang is much greater—1-3/8 inches —thereby facilitating "thumbing" and rapid manual changes. Because the manuals overhang so little on Franck's organ, as the player moves up the terrace of keyboards, his body is inclined forward appreciably more than when seated at an American console.

There is only a quarter of an inch difference between the height of the Cavaillé-Coll bench and the American bench and a quarter of an inch difference between the playing surface of the natural keys of the lowest manual and the middle natural key of the pedalboard.

Bearing in mind that the lowest manual on the American console is the Choir (or Positive) the playing surface of the principal keyboard, the Great, is 2-3/4 inches higher than on Franck's organ.

The most noticeable difference between the two consoles is the relationship of the pedal sharp keys to the manuals. If a plumbline is dropped from the edge of the natural keys of the lowest manual (the Grand-Orgue on Franck's organ) to the center of the pedalboard, the distance between the base of that line and the front end of middle 'D♯ of the pedalboard is 13/16 of an inch. On American organs the pedal keys have been moved forward to give the organist a more natural position. The end of the pedal sharp key nearest the organist has been placed ten inches back of the front line of the Choir keys. The extreme backward position of the pedal sharp keys on Franck's organ gives the player a tendency to pitch forward. He must, therefore, move the bench further back in order to utilize the heel as

_____

[3] Revised Report on the Standardization of the Console. Approved by the Council of the American Guild of Organists, 11 December 1961.

well as the toe in pedal playing. At first glance one would expect Franck to have used practically an "all toes" pedal technique (as did his pupil, Charles Tournemire). However, it is evident from the examples he left us that Franck used the heel almost as frequently as the toe.

THE SPECIFICATIONS

The first specification for the organ of Sainte-Clotilde is contained in a proposal drawn up by the builder Aristide Cavaillé-Coll. It is dated 21 January 1853.[4] Since César Franck was not appointed organist of the church until 1857 and because the existing files relative to this organ contain no correspondence between its builder and Franck, it is logical to assume that Franck had no part in drawing up the specification.

With the exception of the extension of the range of the Pédale from , , C − 'C to , , C − 'D there is no difference between the 1853 proposal and the last record we have of the organ—the third statement of work completed (submitted by Cavaillé-Coll to M. Ballu, the architect), dated 12 July 1858. This statement lists 40 stops, 10 pédales de combinaison and 2,484 pipes.[5]

A notice which appeared the week after the inauguration of the organ stated:

> This instrument was to be as large as possible in relation to the size of the church, namely with 46 stops on three manuals and pedal, having 14 composition pedals and 2, 796 pipes.[6]

Four years later "the organ in Sainte-Clotilde, dedicated 19 December 1859, contains 46 stops."[7] Between the statement of work completed of 12 July 1858 and the dedication of the organ a year and a half later, six stops, four pédales de combinaison and 312 pipes were added to the original scheme. These additions were made after César Franck had assumed his duties as organist of Sainte-Clotilde.[8]

[4] Douglass, *Cavaillé-Coll*, I, 115.

[5] *Ibid.*

[6] *La France musicale* XXIII/52 (25 Dec. 1859) 507.

[7] Abbé Pierre Henri Lamazou, *Étude sur l'orgue monumental de Saint-Sulpice et la facture d'orgue moderne* (Paris: Repos, n.d.) 57.

[8] See Douglass, *Cavaillé-Coll*, I, 139.

The first published specification of the organ of Sainte-Clotilde[9] appears in Albert Schweitzer's monograph *Deutsche und französische Orgelbaukunst und Orgelkunst*,[10] published 47 years after the organ was built and 16 years after Franck's death. By comparing this stoplist with that of Cavaillé-Coll's 1858 statement of work completed we can determine the stops which were added and the changes which were made during Franck's tenure.

	Cavaillé-Coll, 1858		Schweitzer, 1906
	PÉDALE		PÉDALE
		32	Quintaton
16	Contrebasse or Flûte ouverte	16	Contrebasse
8	Basse or Flûte ouverte	8	Flûte
4	Octave	4	Octave
16	Bombarde	16	Bombarde
		16	Basson
8	Trompette	8	Trompette
4	Clairon	4	Clairon

[9] Not only do we not have a nineteenth-century copy of the original specification, but changes were made to the organ during the seventy-year span and tenure of three organists—from its inauguration in 1859 until Charles Tournemire drastically altered its design in 1933. At that time a new console was provided, the Récit was considerably enlarged, some stops transferred from one division to another (ten stops were added, comprising some seventeen ranks of pipes), and the wind pressure of the Positif was reduced. Previously the Grand-Orgue and Positif, in addition to having almost identical specifications, were almost the same degree of loudness and were on the same level inside the organ. The Positif's function as a kind of secondary Grand-Orgue explains, in part, some of Franck's registrations. (Jean-Louis Coignet, *Letter to the author* (Cháteauneuf-de-Bargis, 15 Sept. 1981).

[10] Albert Schweitzer, *Deutsche und französische Orgelbaukunst und Orgelkunst*, 49. This work was actually written in the autumn of 1905 as Schweitzer mentions in his 1914 essay *À propos de la discussion sur la facture d'orgues* (Paris: L'Orgue, Cahiers et Mémoires, No. 22, 1979, 17).

additional changes to the organ included the manual compass being extended to 51 notes, the pedal to 32 notes & 16' stops added to the manuals & pedal.

GRAND-ORGUE

16	Montre
16	Bourdon
8	Montre
8	Flûte harmonique
8	Viole de gambe
8	Bourdon
4	Prestant
4	Octave
4	Viole d'amour
3	Quinte
2	Doublette
IV	Fourniture
III	Cymbale
16	Bombarde
8	Trompette
4	Clairon

GRAND-ORGUE

16	Montre
16	Bourdon
8	Montre
8	Flûte harmonique
8	Viole de ganbe
8	Bourdon
4	Prestant
4	Octave
3	Quinte
2	Doublette
	Plein jeu
16	Bombarde
8	Trompette
4	Clairon

POSITIF

8	Montre
8	Salicional
8	Bourdon
4	Prestant
4	Flûte douce
3	Quinte
2	Doublette
V	Plein jeu
8	Trompette
8	Cromorne

POSITIF

16	Bourdon
8	Montre
8	Flûte harmonique
8	Salicional
8	Gambe
8	Bourdon
4	Prestant
4	Flûte octaviante
3	Quinte
2	Doublette
	Plein jeu
8	Trompette
8	Clarinette
4	Clairon

RÉCIT

8	Flûte harmonique
8	Flûte douce
8	Viole d'amour
4	Flûte octaviante
2	Octavin
8	Trompette harmonique
8	Basson-hautbois
8	Voix humaine

RÉCIT

8	Flûte harmonique
8	Bourdon
8	Viole de gambe
8	Voix céleste
4	Flûte octaviante
2	Octavin
8	Trompette
8	Basson-hautbois
8	Voix humaine
4	Clairon

A comparison of the two stoplists shows ten changes made to the original tonal scheme of 1858. These comprise the following: (a) combination of the two mixtures of the Grand-Orgue into one Plein jeu; (b) elimination of the 4' Viole d'amour (perhaps moved to the Récit where, tuned sharp, it created the Voix céleste); and (c) addition of eight ranks of pipes:

Pédale	32' Quintaton	27 pipes
	16' Basson	27 pipes
Positif	16' Bourdon	54 pipes
	8' Flûte harmonique	54 pipes
	8' Gambe	54 pipes
	4' Clairon	54 pipes
Récit	8' Voix céleste	42 pipes[11]
	4' Clairon	54 pipes

366 pipes

- 54 pipes (Viole d'amour)

312 total pipes added

The addition of the eight new stops, the other modifications, and a computation of the number of pipes in the revised specification equal exactly the report in *La France musicale*. But the fact remains that a copy of the organ specification contemporary with Franck's tenure does not survive and "all record of repairs and alterations, at least up to the time of Franck's death in 1890, has been lost or destroyed."[12]

Because of the absence of an original source for the specification of the organ of Sainte-Clotilde, we have reconstructed it by comparing nine published stoplists. These have been chosen because they represent either the earliest printed source or because they have been furnished by a person closely associated with the organ. The sources for these stoplists are Charles Tournemire (who succeeded Gabriel Pierné

[11] Originally the céleste rank extended the full compass of the manuals, i.e., there were as many pipes as there were keys. The organ which Cavaillé-Coll designed in 1845, but never built, for Saint-Eustache, was to have had both a Voix céleste and an Unda maris on the Récit, each rank of 54 pipes. His organ in Saint-Vincent-de-Paul (1852) had a Voix céleste of 54 pipes on the Grand-Orgue. But by the late 1850's Cavaillé-Coll had established the traditional range for the céleste rank: , C − ' ' 'F, as in the 1859 organ of Saint-Hippolyte à Poligny. See the article "L'orgue de l'église de St-Hippolyte," *La Flûte Harmonique*, No. 2 (1976) 12. Coignet concurs that the Sainte-Clotilde Voix céleste stopped at, C. (Letter to the author, 15 Sept. 1981).

[12] Douglass, *Cavaillé-Coll*, I, 137.

Sainte-Clotilde, Organ Console: Manuals

Koos Schippers

to the post of organist titulaire in 1898 and remained until his death in 1939) and two of his assistants—Joseph Bonnet ("It was my good fortune to know the organ at Sainte-Clotilde thoroughly, for during my first years as a student in Paris, while assistant to Charles Tournemire, I played it constantly."[13]) and Maurice Duruflé who was his assistant in 1920—and various musicians who wrote about the organ: Albert Schweitzer, Jean Huré, Félix Raugel and Flor Peeters,[14] to whom the original Cavaillé-Coll console was bequeathed by Tournemire.

These sources disagree on several points: names of certain stops, number of ranks comprising the mixtures and two of the pédales de combinaison. Chart I below describes all of the discrepencies among the cited sources.

For a clue to the reasons for the variations in the stoplists we might examine the console itself. Plates 14 and 15 (pp. 64 and 66) detail each stop jamb.

Chart I
Stop Discrepancies in Eight Sources

		Cavaillé-Coll	Bonnet	Schweitzer	Raugel	Peeters	Huré	Tournemire	Duruflé
Pédale	32' Quintaton (Q) Sousbasse (S)	-	S	Q	Q	S	S	S	S
Pédale	8' Flûte (F) Basse (B)	B	F	F	F	B	B	B	B
Grand-Orgue	Plein jeu (ranks)	VII	VI	-	-	-	-	VI	VI
Positif	8' Salicional (S) Unda maris (Um)	-	S	S	S	Um	Um	Um	Um
Positif	Plein jeu (ranks)	V	V	-	-	-	-	-	V
Positif	8' Cromorne (Cr) Clarinette (Cl)	Cr	Cr	Cl	Cl	Cl	Cl	Cl	Cl

[13] Bonnet, "Preface," 2.

[14] M. Peeters was "associated" with Tournemire but never studied with him. See *The Diapason* (July 1973) 2.

Sainte-Clotilde, Organ Console: Left stop jamb   Koos Schippers

SOURCES

Cavaillé-Coll: In Douglass, *Cavaillé-Coll*, I, 130.
Bonnet, "Preface," 3.
Schweitzer, *Deutsche und französische Orgelbaukunst und Orgelkunst*, 49.
Raugel, *Les Grandes Orgues de Paris*, 206.
Flor Peeters, "The Organ Works of César Franck, *Music*, V/8 (August 1971) 22.
Jean Huré, *L'Esthétique de L'Orgue* (Paris: Senart, 1923) 81-2.
Charles Tournemire, "Notice" in the program for the *Inauguration du Grand Orgue de la Basilique Ste.-Clotilde de Paris* (13 June 1933). In Douglass, *Cavaillé-Coll*, I, 141.
Maurice Duruflé, "Notice," *Les Trois Chorals de César Franck*. Révision et annotations de Maurice Duruflé (Paris: Durand, 1973).

The name of each stop was engraved on an enamel disc which was glued into the face of the wooden shank which drew the stop. A study of these discs reveals several different styles of lettering—an indication that many of the discs have been replaced. The names of the stops upon which sources disagree are among those whose typeface differs from the original Cavaillé-Coll script. The 32' Sousbasse, 8' Basse, 8' Unda maris, and 8' Clarinette are all engraved in identical Roman type—different from the original script lettering. The two Plein jeux appear to be original but out of place. The Plein jeu harmonique is among the Grand-Orgue stops instead of among those of the Positif. Unfortunately, the number of ranks does not appear on the disc.

The differences in nomenclature of the stops in the specifications are largely a question of semantics. Cavaillé-Coll variously labeled his 32' stopped flues "Sousbasse," "Bourdon" or "Quintaton"; the 8' open flue, "Flûte" and, rarely, "Basse."

Every organ known to have been played by Franck (with the exception of Saint-Jacques-du-Haut-Pas which had no Positif) had a Cromorne on the Positif—and five of those organs had, in addition, a Clarinette on another division. It is unlikely that as early as 1859 Cavaillé-Coll would have called the Cromorne "Clarinette." His proposal and subsequent statements refer to it as a Cromorne.

The Unda maris is frequently substituted for the Positif Salicional in published specifications of the Sainte-Clotilde organ. An undulating stop similar to the Voix céleste, the Unda maris began to appear on most of Cavaillé-Coll's Positif divisions after the early 1860's. Indeed, the organ of Saint-Sulpice (1862) is the first known inclusion of this stop. Bonnet, Schweitzer and Raugel maintain that the additional narrow-scaled flue on the Positif of the Sainte-Clotilde organ was a Salicional. Other sources disagree.

Sainte-Clotilde, Organ Console: Right stop jamb   Koos Schippers

André Marchal, who played the organ on 15 August 1912, informs us that (by then) an Unda maris was among the stops on the Positif.

What is now called "Salicional" is the former Unda maris of the Positif which was tuned to celeste with the Gambe. The "undulation" was suppressed and the Unda maris transformed and tuned into a Salicional around 1934 when the organ was restored.[15]

If the original stop had been a Salicional, it is probable that between the time when Albert Schweitzer copied the stoplist (before 1906) and when André Marchal played the organ (1912), Charles Tournemire tuned the Salicional to celeste with the Gambe. Hence, all subsequent sources list the stop as Unda maris. It is interesting that Tournemire kept the Unda maris for over twenty years before tuning it back to unison pitch during the 1933 rebuild.

The composition and number of ranks in the original mixtures of the organ remain speculative. Jean Fellot maintains that the Fourniture IV and Cymbale III of the Grand-Orgue were combined into a VII-rank Plein jeu classique.[16] Yet Bonnet, Duruflé and Tournemire, all well-acquainted with the organ, list the mixture of the Grand-Orgue as VI ranks.

An original enamel insert engraved "Plein jeu harmonique" is present on the original console. Although found among the stops of the Grand-Orgue, it is obviously misplaced and belongs with the stops of the Positif. It is almost certain that the Positif V-rank Plein jeu would have been reconstituted as a III-VI Plein jeu harmonique soon after the organ's completion. The discrepancy exists because the number of ranks in a mixture did not appear on the stops of Cavaillé-Coll organs.

The Plein jeu harmonique, introduced in the Positif, was unique to

[15] André Marchal, Letter to the author, (Paris, 18 May 1980). Marchal served with Joseph Bonnet and Félix Raugel on the commission which approved the rebuilt organ in 1933.

[16] Jean Fellot, "Chronologie de l'oeuvre de Cavaillé-Coll," *Orgues Historiques*, No. 11 (Paris: C. C. P. Harmonie du Monde, 1965) 19. This combination is not without historical precedent. Georges Lhôte writes ("Remarks on the French Organ," *ISO-Information*, No. 1, Feb. 1969, 82): "The practice of drawing the Fourniture and Cymbale as one stop became more frequent as time went on and was especially typical of the late 1700's when the name Plein jeu was adopted for this combined register." Coignet (Letter to the author, 15 Sept. 1981) writes that ". . . after examining the pipework, I think Fellot is right. New windchests were provided when the organ was electrified. It is now impossible to determine what existed previous to 1933."

Cavaillé-Coll's organs. Although Bonnet and Duruflé list the mixture as V ranks, Fellot points out that the Plein jeu harmonique at Sainte-Clotilde would have been III-VI ranks.[17]

Composed of unisons and quints, the Plein jeu harmonique was basically a cornet without a tierce; unlike a mixture it did not "break back." Cavaillé-Coll developed this "progression harmonique" to compensate for the weak trebles of the reed stops—thus, it increased in ranks and in power as it ascended to the top of the keyboard.[18] The composition of the III-IV rank Plein jeu harmonique was as follows:[19]

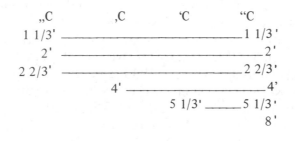

Because the Plein jeu harmonique III-VI has 24 fewer pipes than a five-rank mixture, the total number of pipes in the organ would have been 24 pipes less if the original tabulation were correct.

THE PÉDALES DE COMBINAISON

The list of pédales de combinaison for organ of Sainte-Clotilde has been compiled from six published sources. Chart II shows the ten pédales de combinaison in Cavaillé-Coll's original proposal and those listed in five other sources. Again, the sources do not agree.

Joseph Bonnet,[20] André Marchal[21] and Maurice Duruflé,[22] who

---

[17] According to Georges Lhôte ("Remarks on the French organ," 78): "Where the Plein jeu is concerned, it seems that Cavaillé-Coll had no definite theory; he often made mixtures in the classical manner, but, at the same time, we find the progressing or 'harmonic' Plein jeu . . ."

[18] Fellot, "Chronologie," 19.

[19] *Ibid.*, 29.

[20] Bonnet, "Preface," 3.

[21] Marchal, Letter to the author.

[22] Duruflé, "Notice."

Chart II

The Pédales de Combinaison
As Indicated in Six Published Sources

	Cavaillé-Coll	Bonnet	Huré	Raugel	Tournemire	Peeters
Tirasse Grand-Orgue	X	X	X	X	X	X
Tirasse Positif		X	X	X	X	X
Tirasse Récit			X	X	X	X
Anches Pédale	X	X	X	X	X	X
Octaves graves Grand-Orgue	X	X	X	X	X	X
Octaves graves Positif			X	X	X	X
Octaves graves Récit			X	X		X
Octaves graves Récit au Positif		X			X	
Octaves graves Positif au Grand-Orgue		X				
Anches Grand-Orgue	X	X	X	X	X	X
Anches Positif	X	X	X	X	X	X
Anches Récit	X	X	X	X	X	X
Grand-Orgue sur machine (Introduction)				X		
Positif au Grand-Orgue	X	X	X	X	X	X
Récit au Positif		X	X	X	X	X
Récit au Grand-Orgue	X					
Trémolo	X	X	X	X	X	X
Expression de Récit	X	X	X	X	X	X
Total	10	13	14	15	14	14

SOURCES

Aristide Cavaillé-Coll, *Devis IV*, No. 584 (21 Jan. 1853). In Douglass, *Cavaillé-Coll*, 119–20.

Bonnet, "Preface," 3.

Huré, *L'Esthétique de l'Orgue*, 82.
Raugel, *Les Grandes Orgues de Paris,* 206.
Tournemire, "Notice." In Douglass, *Cavaillé-Coll,* I, 141.
Peeters. "The Organ Works of César Franck," 22.
  A photograph of the console showing the pédales de combinaison (with new labels) appears in Gallois, *Franck,* 69.

---

were acquainted with the original Franck console before 1923, have stated that there was no Tirasse Récit. But the four sources which list Tirasse Récit were published after 1923. We may assume, then, that this Tirasse did not exist on the organ which Franck knew but was added by Charles Tournemire in the 1920's.[23] Note on Chart III how infrequent was the presence of any Tirasse other than that of the Grand-Orgue. None of Cavaillé-Coll's organs in Paris had a Tirasse Récit and, indeed, Sainte-Clotilde was his first organ in the French capital with a Tirasse Positif.

   Franck's organ was the first built by Cavaillé-Coll to have Octaves graves on all three manuals. Three of the sources used in Chart II list these as Octaves graves Grand-Orgue, Octaves graves Positif, and Octaves graves Récit. Tournemire designates two (and Bonnet one) as intra-manual couplers, i.e., operating between two manuals. As discussed in Chapter IV, the Octaves graves was a sub-octave coupler affecting the pitch of its own manual. The same combination could be coupled to another manual, but this was done through the unison *accouplement*—the mechanical action transferred whatever was playing on one division to another. If whatever combination was fixed on the Récit, including the Octaves graves, would be transferred to the Positif with the Récit au Positif, a sub-octave inter-manual coupler would have been redundant. Therefore, "Octaves graves Récit au Positif" and "Octaves graves Positif au Grand-Orgue" must be interpreted

[23] The Tirasse Récit was added to the organ of Saint-Sulpice in 1903 (Raugel, *Les Grandes Orgues de Paris*, 147) and to the organ of Notre-Dame in 1932 (Pierre J. Hardouin, *Le Grand Orgue de Notre-Dame-de-Paris* [Chambray-les-Tours: Bärenreiter, 1973] 40). Hans Brink and Paul Peeters ("Het orgel van César Franck in de Ste. Clotilde: 'Continuing story' of prijsvraag voor organisten?" *Het Orgel* [Feb. 1983] 35) have described their examination of the inner mechanism of the original console in Flor Peeters' studio. They note that the first three slots in the kickboard have been altered. The tracker levers behind the second slot have been extended to the first slot, (i.e., Tirasse Grand-Orgue has been moved over), the third slot extended to the second (i.e., Tirasse Positif has been moved over) and the new Tirasse Récit has been connected to the pédale de combinaison in the third slot. They conclude that the empty first slot was originally "Effet d'orage"- the first pédale de combinaison on virtually all of Cavaillé-Coll's organs of the period.

Chart III

25 Organs of three manuals or more, built or rebuilt by Cavaillé-Coll between 1838 and 1868

	Manuals	Grand-Orgue	Positif	Récit	Grand-Orgue sur Machine	Octaves graves
			Tirasses			
1838 Paris, Notre-Dame-de-Lorette	3	X				
1841 Paris, Saint-Denis	3	X			X	
1842 Paris, Saint-Roch	4	X				G
1845 Ajaccio, Cathédrale	3	X				
1846 Paris, La Madeleine	4	X				GB
1846 Saint-Brieuc, Cathédrale	4	X			X	
1847 Quimper, Cathédrale	3	X				
1849 Bayonne, Cathédrale*	3	X				
1850 Toulouse, Saint-Étienne	3	X			X	RG
1851 Saint-Germain-en-Laye, Saint-Germain	3	X				
1852 Paris, Saint-Vincent-de-Paul	3	X				GP
1852 Carcassonne, Cathédrale	4	X			X	
1857 Paris, Saint-Merry	3	X			X	G
1858 Bergues, Saint-Martin, *(Perpignan Cathédrale)*	3 4	X			X	G All
1860 Nancy, Cathédrale	3	X	X	X	X	G
1861 Paris, Saint-Thomas-d'Aquin	3	X			X	
1862 Bayeux, Cathédrale	3	X			X	G
1862 Saint-Dizier, Notre-Dame	3	X			X	G
1862 Paris, Saint-Sulpice	5	X			X	All
1863 Paris, Saint-Étienne-du-Mont	3	X			X	R
1864 Versailles, Cathédrale	3	X			X	R
1864 Lyon, Saint-François-de-Sales	3	X	X	X	X	GPR
1864 Auch, Cathédrale*	3	X	X			G
1867 Paris, Saint-Denis-Saint-Sacrement	3	X			X	G
1868 Paris, Cathédrale-de-Notre-Dame	5	X			X	All

EXPLANATION OF CHART III

An asterisk (*) represents an organ for which a proposal was submitted but which was never built.

The Octaves graves are abbreviated thus:

G   Grand-Orgue
B   Bombarde
P   Positif
R   Récit
All The two five-manual organs had Octaves
     graves on all manuals.

Because of lack of specific information, four organs were not included. These were:

Notre-Dame-de-Victoires (Paris, 1851)
Saint-Jean (Pézenas, 1853, 3 manuals)
Cathédrale (Saint-Omer, 1855, 4 manuals)
Cathédrale (Perpignan, 1857, 4 manuals)

SOURCES

Douglass, *Cavaillé-Coll.*
Dufourcq, *César Franck et la genèse des premières oeuvres d'orgue.*
Jerôme Faucheur, "Le grand orgue de la cathédrale d'Ajaccio," *L'Orgue*, CL/2 (April-June 1974) 50.
Fellot, "Chronologie de l'oeuvre de Cavaillé-Coll," 18-22.
François Sabatier, *La Palette sonore de Cavaillé-Coll* (Paris: Revue "Jeunesse et Orgue," 1979).

---

as errors which should be corrected to read "Octaves graves Récit" and "Octaves graves Positif."

Bonnet lists only thirteen pédales de combinaison,[24] and if we eliminate the Tirasse Récit from Huré, Tournemire and Peeters, they likewise total thirteen. A fourteenth pédale is listed by Félix Raugel as "Grand-Orgue Introduction." It appeared as "Grand-Orgue sur machine" in an earlier stoplist of the Sainte-Clotilde organ drawn up by Flor Peeters.[25] As is noted in Chart III, by the time of the construction of the Sainte-Clotilde organ the "Grand-Orgue Introduction" (or "sur machine") was a standard feature on Cavaillé-Coll's instruments. Coignet[26] points out that, while most Cavaillé-Coll organs fitted with Barker levers have a "Grand-Orgue Introduction," this device is useful only when one is able to couple both the Positif and the Récit to the Grand-Orgue. This not being the case with the Sainte-Clotilde organ, it

[24] As does Schweitzer (*Deutsche und französische Orgelbaukunst und Orgelkunst*, 49), although without enumerating them: "13 Koppeln und Kombinationszuge."

[25] Flor Peeters, *Ars Organi, Pars III* (Bruxelles: Schott, 1954) 91.

[26] Coignet, Letter to the author.

is highly unlikely that such a coupler existed on that instrument. Now, with the new evidence recently published by Brink and Peeters, the addition of the *Orage* brings the total of the *pédales de combinaison* to fourteen—the number mentioned in the first published account of the organ—in *La France musicale.*[27]

TONAL CHARACTERISTICS

For an appreciation of the tonal characteristics of the organ which inspired César Franck we must turn to verbal descriptions because the tonal qualities of the organ of Sainte-Clotilde, as well as most of the other major Parisian organs, have been altered from their original "symphonic" conception to conform with the "neo-classic" ideals of the organ reform movement which has swept the organ world over the last fifty years. Kurt Lueders wrote that

> ...twentieth-century modifications invariably lead to petty and futile bickering about whether such-and-such a sound is still the same as when so-and-so heard and played and wrote for it. All that can be said for certain in the end—and all that need be said—is that these instruments have been wantonly altered to conform to modern ideals and are no longer the same ones their creator and original users knew. (Indeed, undeniable presence of original pipework cannot offset equally apparent revoicing, as well as new winding systems, interior layouts and generalized electric action, not to mention occasional use of inferior materials.)[28]

The 78-rpm recordings made by Charles Tournemire in 1930 are all that remain of the sound of the organ that César Franck heard.

From the amount and variety of descriptions of its tonal characteristics, the Récit was the most astounding division. Containing but ten stops, it lacked a 16' stop, a principal and a mixture.

> The quality of the Récit was something of a miracle. Undoubtedly, a number of technical reasons contributed to this: the dimensions of the swell box, the responsiveness of the shutters, its location at the back of the organ case, the large sonorous space surrounding the box on all sides giving it an extraordinary reasonance, the acoustics of the church and, above all, the genius of the builder. All these factors produced a miracle.[29]

[27] *La France musicale* XXIII/52 (25 Dec. 1859) 507.

[28] Kurt Lueders, "Amours, Délices et Grandes Orgues, Part V," *Music* X/4 (April 1976) 34.

[29] Maurice Duruflé, "Mes souvenirs sur Tournemire et Vierne," *L'Orgue*, No. 162 (April–June 1977) 4.

Goodrich's general statement—"The Récit is a manual of ample resources and great power when the box is open, affecting materially the whole ensemble of the organ."[30] —accurately describes the Récit of the organ of Sainte-Clotilde. André Marchal commented that

> . . . the Récit on Franck's instrument was very small, sounding very well when the box was open, but when closed the reeds would disappear behind the foundation stops of the other manuals.[31]

Dufourcq adds that "The marvelous swell box of the Récit enveloped all that it enclosed with mystery and poetry."[32]

This phenomenon was well understood by Franck who frequently calls for the tutti of the Récit coupled to the 16' and 8' Fonds of the Grand-Orgue and Positif. In such a combination Duruflé writes that:

> . . . [the] Récit took on surprising prominence. Due to the excellent responsiveness of the swell shutters, sometimes the full ensemble surged to the forefront, sometimes it ebbed, allowing the Fonds 16– 8 to predominate . . . What more ideal sonority could one desire than that of the ensemble of Récit stops for translating a thought which had been precisely inspired by these timbres?[33]

The timbre of the two solo reeds of the Récit was unique when compared to other similar stops made by Cavaillé-Coll and especially when compared to stops of similar names as constructed by foreign builders. The Basson-hautbois was used by Franck as a solo stop in only one instance: the *Prélude* and *Variation* of Opus 18. And it is strengthened by the addition of the Bourdon and Flûte. Always it is added to the three foundation stops "to render appreciable the nuances produced by the opening and closing of the swell box."[34]

The Trompette, on the other hand, is Franck's preferred solo voice and, as such, appears in five works: *Fantaisie,* Op. 16, *Prière, Cantabile, Choral I* and *Choral III*. This Trompette was small, "almost an Hautbois, of very great finesse and flexibility."[35] It was quite powerful,

---

[30] Goodrich, *The Organ in France*, 22.

[31] André Marchal, "André Marchal talks to Rodney Baldwyn on the occasion of César Franck's 150th birthday," *Organist's Review*, No. 58 (Dec. 1973) 13.

[32] Dufourcq, *Franck*, 19.

[33] Duruflé, "Mes souvenirs," 4.

[34] Cellier, *L'Orgue moderne*, 61.

[35] *Ibid.*, 74.

but with ". . . a light, clear, smooth quality; its use in combination with the Hautbois and foundation stops . . . results in a rich and warm ensemble tone."[36]

A peculiar feature of the Sainte-Clotilde organ was the lack of a 16' Bourdon in the Pédale. Three 16' flue stops on the manuals and three powerful reeds of 16' pitch (one on the Grand-Orgue and two in the Pédale) provided a gravity of tone seldom found in organs today. The single 16' Contrebasse provided the clear bass line at sub-octave pitch. Lynnwood Farnam wrote that ". . . curiously enough the solitary flue answers the purpose so well that so far as I could hear there was little wrong in the matter of balance."[37] As the manuals were coupled to the Pédale and the volume of tone increased, the ensemble ultimately included two stopped and two open doubles.

The organ of Sainte-Clotilde was "noted alike for the distinction and charm of its individual stops as for the power and clarity of its ensemble."[38] Dufourcq's description that "The tutti, incisive and without heaviness, sounded powerful and clear"[39] is qualified by the American organist Marshall Bidwell, who wrote in the early 1920's, "The organ sounded very brilliant, though not particularly loud in proportion to the size of the church."[40]

[36] Bonnet, "Preface," 2.

[37] "A chat with Lynnwood Farnam," *The Musical Times* (August 1923) 544.

[38] Bonnet, "Preface," 2.

[39] Dufourcq, *Franck*, 19.

[40] Marshall Bidwell, "Organ music in Paris churches, Part V," *The American Organist* VI/1 (Jan. 1923) 14.

Charles Tournemire

(at the new console of the rebuilt organ of Saint-Clotilde)

CHAPTER SIX

CÉSAR FRANCK BY CHARLES TOURNEMIRE

ᴖᴖ

INTRODUCTION

On September 5, 1930, Charles Tournemire completed his book on César Franck.[1] It was published the following year by the firm of Delagrave in Paris in their series "Les Grands Musiciens par les maîtres d'aujourd'hui." Like d'Indy, Tournemire had studied with Franck at the Paris Conservatoire and his authoritative comments on Franck's works and personality have the weight of firsthand knowledge.

Born in Bordeaux in 1870, Charles Tournemire entered César Franck's organ class at the Paris Conservatoire in October 1889. In a notebook which he kept to record his students' progress, Franck described the nineteen-year-old boy as an "excellent student," "very gifted," and "a worker."[2] Tournemire studied with Franck for one year. One month after the beginning of the second school year Franck died. Continuing his organ studies under Charles Marie Widor, Franck's successor as professor of organ, Tournemire won the first prize in organ in June 1891.

He studied composition at the Schola Cantorum with Vincent d'Indy and served as organist of Saint-Médard. In December 1897 he was appointed organist of Saint-Nicolas-de-Chardonnet, and eight months

---

[1] Charles Tournemire, *César Franck* (Paris: Delagrave, 1931).

[2] Marcelle Benoit, "César Franck et ses élèves," *L'Orgue*, No. 83 (April–Sept. 1957) 76.

later he succeeded Gabriel Pierné[3] to the post of organist of the Basilica of Sainte-Clotilde, the position held for thirty-two years by César Franck.

Tournemire won recognition as a composer in 1903 with the Prize of the City of Paris for his cantata *The Blood of the Siren*. He was professor of ensemble at the Paris Conservatoire from 1919 until his death in 1939.

His fame, quite apart from his talent as a composer and improviser, has always rested on his great devotion to César Franck. For forty years he was "organist of Franck's church." As a disciple of Franck he conveyed the Franckian tradition to the next generation of organists. In 1930 he made phonograph recordings of Franck's music on the organ of Sainte-Clotilde and wrote his book on Franck.

César Franck is divided into ten chapters: "Reflections on Art," "Mystical Considerations," "Birth of the Franckist Movement," "The Masterpieces," "Organ Music (The Nine Pieces)," "The Three Chorals," "Chamber Music," "César Franck Improvisateur," "The Future," and "César Franck Intime."

In his discussion of Franck's compositions Tournemire restricted himself to the works which had not been extensively analyzed: the organ music, the *Sonata* and the *Quintette*.

A weakness of the book is the author's prose—a style described by a reviewer as "fulminating Hugoese."[4] A brief example will demonstrate the florid, poetic meandering which characterizes the entire work. In speaking of the *Fantaisie*, Op. 16, Tournemire writes:

Une large exposition d'une blancheur de neige, presque entièrement diatonique, donne naissance à un canon d'une pureté confondante sur lequel doucement vient se poser, de manière ailée, l'adorable ligne.[5]	A broad exposition, as white as snow, almost entirely diatonic, becomes a canon of an amazing purity upon which the exquisite melody softly alights as if with wings.

[3] Gabriel Pierné had succeeded to the post of organist of Sainte-Clotilde upon the death of Franck in 1890. He resigned in 1898.

[4] Archibald Farmer, "The Musician's Bookshelf," *The Musical Times* LXXII/1063 (Sept. 1931) 800. In April, 1936 Tournemire visited London and broadcast a recital over the B.B.C. He was asked to write an article on the art of improvisation for *The Listener*. The prose-poem he submitted, in the same style as this book, was felt by the editor to defy translation and appeared in the original French.

[5] Tournemire, *Franck*, 21.

Another weakness is the author's attribution of ecstatic religious inspiration to almost every work of Franck. He shares this trait with other "Franckists" who attempt to give Franck's very subjective music an air of spiritual isolation—to make it "holy." Vincent d'Indy's "Pater Seraphicus" is Tournemire's "Fra Angelico of Sound." When Tournemire saw the *Final* "as a sonorous pyramid reaching toward the Eternal's glorification"[6] or described the *Cantabile* as "the soul's unsatisfied desire—a saint's inner supplications—incessant pleas—faith in divine mercy,"[7] we are reminded of Guy Ropartz who recognized the "theme of faith" motif throughout Franck's works or d'Indy, who wrote of the "mystical significance" of *Psyché* which, "in spite of its antique title, has nothing of the pagan spirit about it . . . but . . . is imbued with Christian grace and feeling."[8]

These reservations aside, we shall now consider the value of this document as the only primary source for the interpretation of the organ music of César Franck. Chapter Five, the longest in the book, presents the only detailed analysis of Franck's organ works written by one of his pupils.

Tournemire places great emphasis on rhythmic suppleness and freedom from metronomic strictness. "*Sans rigueur*" is the most frequently encountered qualifying adjective, as is seen in the sampling of interpretive directions given below:

Lento:	according to the performer's inner feelings.
Poco lento:	without dragging, obviously without rigor.
Adagio:	very freely, never hurrying and with great freedom. César Franck played this passage rubato and the respect of metronomic movement would be heresy and absolutely contrary to his intentions.
Adagio:	rejects metronomic movement.
Andante:	the metronomic marking is not strictly observed.
Andantino:	without rigor.
Andantino:	fluctuations of movement impose themselves; with much freedom throughout.
Allegretto poco mosso (*Sonate pour Violon*):	without rigor.

[6] *Ibid.*, 25.

[7] *Ibid.*

[8] d'Indy, *Franck*, 173.

Slow tempi are not too slow and we are cautioned against playing fast movements too fast:

Andantino sostenuto:	a reserved ♩ = 66.
Quasi allegretto:	Generally, the staccato part is executed at a dizzying speed which completely destroys the balance of the work.
Allegro non troppo e maestoso:	♩ = 80, without rigor. . . .
Allegro:	♩ = 96, yet very reserved.
Allegro (second movement of the *Sonate pour Violon*):	the usual confusion which results from an excess of speed is not in the spirit of the composer. César Franck himself interpreted it thus: ♩ = 112.

Tutti and fortissimo passages, even when not so marked by the composer, are to be interpreted broadly and grandly. Tournemire usually directs that the endings of pieces should be played "sempre largamente," "très largement," "largement," or "più largo":

Allegro non troppo e maestro:	in a grandiose and solid manner.
Allegro maestoso:	with grandeur.
Poco animato, *con fantasia*:	with much freedom and imagination. The playing ought to be penetrating and profound . . . the "build-up" must be played freely. Let us throw the metronome away.
Largamente:	must be played with grandeur.

Throughout *César Franck*, Tournemire advocates rhythmic flexibility, cautions against excesses in tempi, whether too slow or too fast, and faithfully adheres to all interpretive markings which appear in the original Durand edition prepared by Franck. Tournemire has provided us with a unique catalogue of interpretive directions written, in turn, as a devoted pupil and an eminent musician.

TRANSLATION OF CHAPTER V OF *CÉSAR FRANCK* BY CHARLES TOURNEMIRE

| Organ Music: The Nine Pieces |

Since the works of the master have been scrupulously analyzed in many important writings, we will confine ourselves to an examination of the organ works, the *Sonate*, and the *Quintette*. In so doing we shall give the *intentions of the composer himself*. Twelve organ pieces represent Franck's contribution to the literature of the noblest of instruments. Three periods separate them: 1860 to 1862 brought us the *Six Pièces: Fantaisie, Grande Pièce symphonique, Prélude, Fugue et Variation, Pastorale, Prière, Final.∥Fantaisie en la, Cantabile*, and *Pièce héroïque* were composed in 1878. Finally, very near his death, the master sketched and completed in only three weeks, those imperishable monuments: the *Trois Chorals*.

The *Fantaisie in C* is an easily analyzed work. A broad exposition, as white as snow, almost entirely diatonic, becomes a canon of an amazing purity upon which the exquisite melody softly alights as if with wings:

A simple "transition" in diminished seventh chords [m. 57] [9] leads to a central section (F minor). Curiously, this section forms a sort of "little republic": it constitutes a pastorale which can easily be isolated. It is distinguished by a writing as elegant as one would wish; the graceful voice-crossings make it sound picturesque. The *Quasi lento* is a "musical" rest. It paves the way for the ineffable peroration: an intensely peaceful little poem.

First part: *Poco lento* (without dragging) ♩ = 66, obviously without rigor. The "transition," very freely, a bit dramatic and rather quickly. The "pastorale," about ♩ = 76, very flexible. *Quasi lento*, simply, stressing the big chords. Then, the concluding, infinitely calm *Adagio* rejects metronomic rhythm, thank God! Retrospection, contemplation—that is the *Adagio*.

[9] Page numbers have been changed to measure numbers for ease in location in all editions of Franck's works.

The *Grande Pièce symphonique* is fundamentally a sonata; the divisions are distinct: *Introduction* and *Allegro non troppo e maestoso* —*Andante*— *Allegro* (in the spirit of a *Scherzo*)—return of the *Andante* —several references to previous material and then a broad conclusion.

One might consider this piece as the first "romantic" sonata conceived for the organ. When Franck played it at the inauguration of the old organ of Saint-Eustache there was a general astonishment ("astonishment" is, of course, used in a derogatory sense).

Nevertheless, the plan was essentially classic, Beethovenian; but by this time, the harmonies are characteristic and this is precisely the reason why the "complicated polyphony" distressed everyone. One could not define the exact philosophical meaning of these numerous pages; yet it is not unreasonable to think that the motivation derives from the contemplation and resultant inner joy of self-fulfillment at overcoming the obstacles to the ideal. The *Andantino serioso*, around ♩ = 69. All of this beautifully sonorous section which precedes the *Allegro non troppo e maestoso*—with grandeur and steadiness. The ¢ about ♩ = 80, without rigor in numerous "spots." The *Andante*, written in a mellowness characteristic of the composer, about ♩ = 60 —not strictly observed. The *Scherzo-Allegro* is in 2/4 time, a very reserved   ♩ = 96. The diverse elements which follow should be the same as in the movements previously indicated. Finally, the concluding *Grand Choeur* (with the beautiful serpentine figure in the pedal), executed in a grandiose and solid manner,   ♩ = 80. Begin the exposition of the fugue ♩ = 60; the following, *animato, ad libitum.*

The *Prélude, Fugue et Variation* constitutes an exquisite composition. Can you not imagine a shepherd piping the beauties of nature without the least hint of paganism? After the exposition, solemn chords overshadow this sweet cantilena . . . The moving Fughetta which follows is a contrapuntal flower, and the reprise [the *Variation*], ornamented with unique "lace," intensifies this music which exhales a perfume of mountain heights. The *Andantino*, around   ♩ = 60—without strictness. The *Lento*— according to the performer's inner feelings. The *Allegretto ma non troppo*, around   ♩ = 88.

Franck loved the following phrase:

The *Variation*, as in the beginning—clearly and unhurried and on the tips of the fingers. At the end—stress:

This is almost Bach.

Those who have not lived in the intimacy of Franck's heart will have to remember the following advice regarding the interpretation of the "extensible" phrase which he so often used in his works. Here is an example:

One finds an "extramusical" meaning, a leap into the beyond.

The *Pastorale* is a charming piece which in structure approximates the *Fantaisie in C*: the middle sections are the same—in the sub-dominant. A slight difference: there are no transitional sections. Exposition of the calm theme—development—and a return to this theme. Nothing simpler. Generally the staccato section is executed at a dizzying speed which completely destroys the balance of the work.

Andantino: ♩. = 58; *Quasi allegretto*: ♩ = 100. The exposition of the fugue—a little less quickly.

The *Prière* is the most remarkable of the six pieces. It is a broad fresco of a single theme. A profound thought excellently expressed. It seems as though the phrase in itself is not able to satisfy man's comprehension. Truly, it [the phrase] grows in the soul's interior and transfigures itself on high.

The central "peace," a sort of recitative, provides the necessary *détente*. Psychologically, this is quite true. After this "truce" the main theme returns with intensity and envelops itself in flames.

Andante sostenuto: a reserved ♩ = 66. The central recitative [from m. 114] with great freedom. From m. 149 animate, then a ritard before the recapitulation: ♩ = 66. Search for the intensity of expression which such music requires. The peroration is in the realm of fantasy.

The *Final in B-flat* is constructed in the manner of a Sonata-Allegro. Notice the key of the second theme: F-sharp major:

B♭ to A♯ , enharmonic common tones. This second theme is very expansive.

The *Allegro maestoso* ♩ = 132. Tempo fluctuations are left to the discretion of the interpreter. The *Final* must be considered as a sonorous pyramid reaching toward the Eternal's glorification.

The *Fantaisie [in A]* is conceived with great simplicity and is characterized by a contemplative exposition; then a great descending line, exquisitely contoured, appears. The unadorned, thinly textured middle section is a sort of interrupted variation taken from the first theme. Then, starting at m. 198, the "passage" ends *fff*. Here there is a combination of the two main elements of the work.

The delicate ending dies away like a sweet mystical thought faintly etched.

Andantino: ♩ = 88. Rhythmic fluctuations are inherent. Much freedom throughout. After the *Très largement*, at *pp* (m. 214) return to the initial tempo, but infinitely calm. From m. 254, a very moderate tempo, slowing down until the end.

The *Cantabile* is a masterpiece: the soul's unsatisfied desire—a saint's inner supplications—incessant pleas—faith in divine mercy. This page—one of Franck's most remarkable—is a simple melody, softly contoured, like the shore of a lake. The canon:

is one of the most beautiful. It blooms in full clarity. The peroration, re-
quiring total concentration, is the perfect expression of suavity. General
tempo   ♩ = 69. The "rest" . . . according to the performer's feelings.

The *Pièce héroïque* is an epic poem. Was he writing of the glorification of heroes or of a personal victory? We prefer the second hypo-
thesis.

The use of "beating" chords at the beginning is rather curious. One
must only consider the beauty of the dramatic line. It tries to be
menacing but doesn't succeed. With increasing mournfulness (from m.
47) it implores the Eternal for help.

Hastily we arrive at the *"Oasis"* in B major, a momentary haven
from anxiety: appeasement, rather than a definite victory for the
vibrant and believing being.

The *Allegro maestoso*:   ♩ = 96. From m. 34, insistent. Play the left
hand part from m. 47 very legato and even. From m. 60 make a ca-
dence of the descending line which precedes the return to the initial
theme.

The middle section, less quickly. From m. 109 progressively ani-
mated and restless. Finally, the repeat of the opening theme. At the *ff*
(m. 151) with grandeur. The end is a song of interior triumph.

TRANSLATION OF CHAPTER Vbis OF *CÉSAR FRANCK*
BY CHARLES TOURNEMIRE

The Three Chorals

Organ music's highest expression is manifested in the *chorale*. The
refined style which flows through it assigns a special place to it. It is
not only a question of writing; the impact is more elevated. It is the
expression of the state of a particular soul . . . .

From the moment the composer enters this incense-perfumed
temple he feels himself filled with dignity: his prayerful soul is imbued
with clarity.

We witness this in the works of Scheidt, Pachelbel, Buxtehude, and J. S. Bach (the master of masters): simple chorales, ornamented chorales, chorale fantasies.

What is most remarkable about Buxtehude is the free treatment of the "Protestant melody"; two of his most important works in this style: *Magnificat, Te Deum*. In these monuments the plainchant is naturally the most important (without meter—each note is changed into a half note). What sumptuous counterpoint: flamboyant rose windows, alleluia-like frescos.

Undoubtedly, we see there the origin of the vast conception of the angelic master: the "Latin" chorale—more supple than the Lutheran hymn.

Before leaving the "old" masters, it is fitting to salute with love and respect, the *Cantor* of Leipzig.

The freedom of conception and the fantasy carried by the ornamented melody (once so criticized—under the pretext that the melody was obscured) makes this complicated art, unequaled in the power of realization, a model always present in our minds.

The chorale seemed to have been exhausted. Then after a deep sleep of about one-hundred-forty years, a bold enterprise marked a very important epoch in the history of music *par excellence*: there was a most interesting mixture of two forms: the *chorale variation* and the *Beethovenian fantasia* (of the late quartets).

This genial combination resulted in the advancement of the developments around the chorale.

A new and glorious creation had just been born. It was exploited by César Franck.

Analyzing the *Three Chorals* is pleasant for us because we cannot forget the emotion we experienced the day we heard these magnificent works played by the master on the piano in his home. Our duty was to play the pedal part "*à la main.*" An extraordinary première! It was then that the impressions, which we translate here, were imprinted in our mind and heart.

Choral in E major[10]

NB: The footnotes in this chapter are additional comments by Charles Tournemire from his *Précis d'exécution, de registration et d'improvisation à l'orgue* (Paris: Eschig, 1936)

---

[10] This choral is the most richly harmonized of the three. The long prelude, very difficult to make legato (unless one couples the manuals to the pedal), is clearly built on the tonal center of E major which is also that of the choral itself.

"The choral *creates* itself during the course of the prelude," said Franck to us.

(handwritten above "creates": evolves)

This is true.

One might wonder whether the composer had planned the tonality of E major (the key center) from the beginning. And certainly this is consciously planned; the effect is magnificent: a luminous tonal foundation over which the choral places itself in a natural manner.

The secondary elements contained in the prelude, satellites of the choral, group themselves around the principal theme:

Choral

Here are the elements:

At m. 46 place a fermata over the chord on the second beat.[11] The first variation

---

[11] in order to separate the entrance of the choral.

is only an embellishment of the first "satellite," m. 73:

It is an evocation of the choral itself.

At the third beat of m. 80 the second "satellite" appears.

Between m. 87 and m. 102 there is an admirable mixture of the choral element and the beginning passages.

From m. 106 to m. 125: a region of "repose."[12]

The following remarkable embellishment springs from No. 1:

Thusly, until the development in the second variation (beginning at m. 126), with very distinct purpose:

(Fragt. Choral)

The same from m. 153, but enriched by the addition, at m. 160:

[12] a kind of diversion.

From m. 166 beautiful harmonies are built on No. 1; they prepare the return, in G minor, of the choral melody (from which supremely strong "garlands" flow).

Grandiose phrase, divine breath, intensity resulting from genius; extraordinary association of contrapuntal and thematic combinations leading to the reprise (*Organo pleno*) of the choral theme, enveloped, at the very end, by the opening theme transformed in a triumphal sense:

The *Moderato*: ♩ = 69. Emphasize the first variation (beginning at m. 65).[13] From m. 106 to m. 125 with much freedom and imagination.

The second variation, m. 126, should move a little faster.[14] From m. 171, bring out the choral (in G minor).[15] From m. 197, with *increasing warmth* until the *fff* (reprise of the choral). The end, in a ray of glory.

Choral in B minor[16]

The mournful melody, stated in the pedal, unfolds majestically; it then passes to the right hand and thus, alternately, until the end of the exposition at m. 64. A sort of *coda, extension of the first theme*, rather adds to the grandeur of the conception.

The "little *divertissement*" which follows (a little in the spirit of Buxtehude) is an adorable thing of infinite delicacy. It lasts only a moment to allow for the continuation of the *coda*; then it appears,

[13] without hurrying.

[14] lively (*vivante*).

[15] put more weight on the choral.

[16] Sort of a passacaglia. In that this work is closely allied to Buxtehude and J. S. Bach. From the beginning, the solemn theme in the pedal definitely fixes the "*genre.*"

transposed a fourth higher. It fades anew and by virtue of the musician's admirable logic, the final balance of the first part of the work affirms itself softly in the theme of the choral, on the Voix humaine (much to the displeasure of the Jansenists of the organ).

The *largamente con fantasia* is easily violinistic.[17] This is just an aside.

The return of the choral (G minor) is worthy of J. S. Bach: the contrapuntal vestment is of a rarely surpassed elegance. The famous passage:

can be played on two keyboards: the *choral only* on the lower—*all the rest* on the upper. A complex arrangement, evidently, but the clever organist with a sure technique, ought to be able to overcome this great difficulty. The result will be an extraordinary illumination of the melody.

In the E-flat minor passage the playing ought to be penetrating.[18] The progressive "build-up" ("*montée*")—like an equinoctial tide—must be dramatic. The soaring theme leads to the return of the choral: *fff*. The "tapering-off" ("*degradé*") permits the return of *the theme of the extension*,[19] a necessary repetition. The last four measures—a little Schubertian—exhale a singular perfume.

The plan of this movement, in brief, is presented thusly:

---

[17] rather in the style of a violin concerto.

[18] profound.

[19] prepares the return of the extended coda.

> ⌈ Exposition (B minor)—*with extension of the choral.*
> ⌊ Little divertissement.
> ⌈ Second extension.
> ⌊ Little divertissement transposed.
> Third extension.
> *Fantaisie.*
> Return of the choral melody (G minor).
> ⌈ Great "build-up" and, *fff.*
> ⌊ Last manifestation of the choral (B minor).
> — Then, conclusion.

The *Maestoso:* ♩ = 76. (At m. 41 play the pedal legato, the left hand detachée, and make the octaves in the right hand as *cantabile* as possible.)

The little *divertissement,* m. 80, is executed very freely:[20] a slight rubato is inherent. Such, at least, was the interpretation of the composer.

It is evident that the "build-up" must be played freely. The art of extra-musical interpretation is *de rigueur.* Let us throw the metronome away. May the mystical inner flame powerfully manifest itself and may the cathedralesque vaults resound with this overflowing paraphrase of divine love.[21]

Choral in A minor

This is the simplest of the three.
The prelude, influenced by J. S. Bach,

BACH

FRANCK

---

[20] *légèrement rubato.*

[21] Let us try to evoke the splendor of cathedral vaults and let us furnish them with our sonorous and mystical draperies.

has a highly classical style. It is followed by great broken chords which must be played with grandeur. Place a fermata over the A minor chord on the first beat of m. 30 (before the exposition of the choral).[22] At m. 48 the prelude returns in the dominant—the reappearance of the great broken chords—then, the repetition of the choral, always in the dominant, with extensive modification in the transposition—conclusion of this part in A minor. The great chords again, then, stop on the dominant of A.

From the beginning, we have gone from the tonic to the dominant and back again. An extraordinary economy of means. The [tonal] center itself does not move. We remain in A.

The "head" of the admirable expressive garland, which ornaments this central section so magnificently, flows from a fragment of the choral:

An ideal "deduction" influenced by Beethoven. We are in the *Ninth Symphony* . . . but the feeling is different. From m. 117 the garland is grafted onto the choral in an emotional manner. From m. 142 play the pedal theme very pronounced (*très marqué*). At m. 147 the prelude returns over a C-major sixth chord,[23] then, a genial return of the choral melody over an augmented fourth chord. Finally, the brilliant

[22] Generally, one goes on—and it is a grave error!

[23] On the ineffable chord of the sixth (the most beautiful in music) the Bachian element is singularly dramatized.

ending very solidly established on the immovable bass of *A*. A rare eloquence and a grandiose style characterize the last measures.

The *Quasi allegro*: ♩ = 100. Play the *Quasi allegro* (from m. 20) animatedly. The choral (m. 20) in the original tempo.[24] The broken chords at m. 53 and m. 55 — "*sempre largamente*."

Play the middle section in A major (m. 97) very freely: ♪ = 76,[25] never hurrying, and with great freedom. It is a recitative.

The respect of metronomic rhythm would be heresy and *absolutely contrary to Franck's intentions*. We definitely affirm this and will not bear discussion. From m. 119 to m. 146, let yourself go and let the theme expand. At m. 142 play the pedal non-legato: orchestrally, very "Trombone-like."

This is how the composer himself played. The great chords daringly and obtaining a lot of sonority from the instrument.

At m. 147, couple the Récit to the Positif. At the third beat of m. 157 and m. 164 open the swell box 3/4 *on the choral*.

These dramatic effects on two keyboards are very much in the *style* of the master.

The "build up" from m. 168: agitated;[26] the choral: majestically:[27] *fff*. Detach the melody and do not connect the inner parts—even shorten them a little.

It gains thus in luminosity.

The end, *très largement*.[28] elevated in thought.

The *Choral in A minor*, the last work of an angelic musician, is a model of simplicity. It is related *by the intimate theme* to Frescobaldi:[29]

Teccata pour l'élévation.

Centre du Choral . . .

24 ♩ = 100.

[25] *mais en tout liberté.* César Franck played this passage "rubato."

[26] *con fuoco.*

[27] *largement.*

[28] *più largo.*

[29] the other "Fra Angelico of sound!"

It is more *modal* than tonal.

The way is opened to immense possibilities: the Gregorian melody is there, very close. . . . A unique instance in Franck's music.

CHAPTER SEVEN

THE TOURNEMIRE RECORDINGS

~~

In 1930 Charles Tournemire made ten 78-rpm recordings on the organ of the Basilica of Sainte-Clotilde. Five of the discs[1] contained music of César Franck. Besides two pieces from *L'Organiste*, a major organ work from Franck's three creative periods was selected: *Pastorale* from *Six Pièces*, *Cantabile* from *Trois Pièces*, and his last composition, the *Third Choral*.[2]

All of these discs are in the Historical Sound Recordings Collection of Yale University. They are in mint condition with virtually noise-free surfaces. Sound reproduction is superb; there is no distortion.

It is apparent that a great deal of attention to detail and planning preceded the recording sessions. The organ is admirably in tune—more so than most French organs on modern recordings. Side breaks were well thought out and coincide with musical pauses. At no time does one have the feeling that the performer is rushing to "get it all in" before the side ends. Hence, we can be certain that Tournemire's tempi were not dictated by the clock. (Each side of a 12-inch 78-rpm disc can hold up to $4\frac{1}{2}$ minutes of music.)

[1] Polydor 561047 10" Sides A and B: *Cantabile*.
Polydor 561048 10" Side A: *L'Organiste: "Chant de la creuse"* *"Noël angevin."*
Polydor 566057 12" Sides A and B: *Third Choral*.
Polydor 566058 12" Side A: *Third Choral* (conclusion).
Polydor 566059 12" Sides A and B: *Pastorale*.

[2] This recording was awarded the Grand Prix du Disque on May 18, 1931. (Joël-Marie Fauquet, *Catalogue de l'oeuvre de Charles Tournemire* [Genève: Minkoff, 1979] 99)

Microphone placement varies from disc to disc. Softer pieces are recorded close to the organ: one can hear the speech of the pipes, the movement of the organ action, the changing of stops, and the organist's feet on the pedals. For those works employing the full organ, the microphones are moved further away from the organ case.

Registration has been planned with care. Perhaps Tournemire sensed that he was preserving the sounds that inspired César Franck.

Tournemire seems to have been comfortable playing in front of a microphone. Of the eight sides devoted to Franck's music, all but two were issued from the first "take." Side Two of *Cantabile* is the second take. The second side of the *Third Choral* (from m. 80 to m. 117) was issued in two forms: the German pressing, released on the Deutsche Grammophon label (which was distributed in Great Britain) represents the first "take"; the French pressing, on Polydor, records the second "take." The difference is significant: for the first take, heard in the Deutsche Grammophon pressing, Tournemire uses the Hautbois as the solo stop for the Adagio (m. 96); on the second take, released on Polydor, he uses the Trompette. Thus, we are given the opportunity to hear, side by side, the two solo reeds most used by Franck.

Charles Tournemire's recordings constitute a unique legacy of a Franck organ student playing Franck's organ works on Franck's original organ.

It is interesting to note the impression Tournemire's recorded performances made on his contemporaries. His interpretations, which adhere with something less than scrupulous fidelity to the composer's specific intentions as printed in the score, were considered, at the time, to be an almost pedantic approach. We read in a British organ journal a review of Tournemire's recording of the *Third Choral*:

> A record of César Franck's organ at Sainte-Clotilde may rightly be termed historical, and to Polydor belongs the honor of having induced a distinguished pupil of Franck to play one of his master's best known and best loved works. . . . this record is admirable in the sense that the recording has permitted the music to speak for itself. There is an absence of deliberate interpretation, of atmosphere, which so often, in the case of one who listens for the first time to a work, clouds his understanding and appreciation of it. Charles Tournemire has made a record which is quite ideal for the Franck beginner. . . . [3]

[3] A. C. D. de Brisay, "Review of Gramophone Records," *The Organ* X/39 (Jan. 1931) 181.

The freedom in performance to which Tournemire constantly refers in his book, *César Franck*, may be heard on his recordings. It is a rhythmic freedom whose nuances are incapable of being catagorized. For instance, in the following phrase Tournemire stresses the first of the barred sixteenth notes in each measure (in the following examples, notes marked by an asterisk are particularly emphasized—usually by a strong tenuto-like prolongation):

Pastorale, m. 32–34

When this phrase is repeated several times at the end of the piece Tournemire stresses the second sixteenth note, or the secondary accent of each first beat.

Pastorale, m. 170–172

Thus, through variation, the performer achieves an even greater freedom of interpretation than he had advocated in his writings.

The highest note in a phrase is often lengthened. But frequently such a note will not be emphasized. Two beautifully executed, slightly prolonged high notes occur in the following examples.

Third Choral, m. 101

Third Choral, m. 111

Often, a note of short duration on the last half of a weak beat which passes to a strong beat is lengthened:

Cantabile, m. 57–60

In phrases containing notes of mixed values, it is always the notes of shorter duration which are rhythmically prolonged. In this phrase the eighth-note duplets are perceptibly lengthened but the accompaniment under the quarter notes remains rhythmically precise:

Cantabile, m. 76–77

Below the left hand passing notes are considerably prolonged:

Third Choral, m. 64

In the following example, although the sixteenth-note groups are prolonged the eighth notes are strictly observed, so that the freedom of movement is governed by the established rhythm. Even though the sixteenth notes are lengthened, we hear the difference between them and the eighth notes.

Third Choral, m. 114

A melodic motif may be singled out for rhythmic prolongation. Throughout the Adagio of the *Third Choral* a rising figuration, beginning on the second of a group of four sixteenth notes, is lengthened:

Third Choral, m. 107

Third Choral, m. 109

Non-chord tones are frequently stressed. The following unaccented passing tones are singled out and played tenuto:

Third Choral, m. 20-22

Tournemire does not always interpret a fermata as a "hold." Rather it signals the end of a phrase. Usually a fermata is preceded by a ritard, but there are exceptions when Tournemire maintains the tempo steadily up to the end of a phrase.

Ritards are frequent—nearly every phrase has an almost imperceptible ritard. But the original tempo is always resumed at the beginning of the next phrase. If a ritard is not printed in the score, but is indicated in an analogous place, it is observed.

In the *Third Choral*, ritards which are not indicated in the score but which Tournemire observes occur at the following measures: 47, 52, 64, 79, 90, 96, 99, 116 and 173. In the *Pastorale* each phrase is slightly ritarded. Some of the measures in which very obvious unmarked ritards are made are: measure 4, 7, 12, 18, 22, 36, 56, 66, 68, 120 and 141.

Whereas unmarked ritards are interpreted, some of those printed are occasionally ignored! Measures 115 of the *Third Choral* is marked "*Rall.*" Tournemire begins a noticeable accelerando which continues into the next measure. The rallantando occurs at the fourth beat of m. 116.

The performer of today who frequently has to "turn the organ upside down" to obtain sounds which vaguely approximate those of a French organ will be astonished at Tournemire's disregard of Franck's registrational directions. In certain instances a reed stop may be played alone instead of drawn with other stops—perhaps to avoid the "beat" caused by out-of-tune notes. At other times a completely different registration is drawn or certain specifically required couplers are not engaged.

The *Pastorale* begins on the Hautbois of the Récit—the 4' Flûte and 8' Bourdon, indicated by Franck, are not drawn with it. The Récit is not coupled to the Positif so that the phrases played on the Positif (m. 5–8, 13–16, 19–20, and 23–24) are rendered without expression. For the Quasi allegretto section (m. 41), the Trompette and Clairon are the only stops drawn on the Récit. The Hautbois re-enters, by itself, at measure 147. On the first beat of the last measure of the piece, the Hautbois is retired and the Voix céleste is added!

In the *Cantabile* the Hautbois is again heard alone, contrary to Franck's directions: "Jeux de fonds de 8 pieds, Hautbois, Trompette." At m. 43 the Récit is coupled to the Positif, as is specified in the score, but the Positif is not coupled to the Pédale. On the second beat of m. 86 the Hautbois is retired and the last four bars of the *Cantabile* are played on the Voix humaine with Trémolo.

Tournemire omits the manual coupler Récit au Positif at m. 48–56, 80–96, and 147–171 in the *Third Choral.* The Adagio (m. 96) is played either on the Hautbois or Trompette of the Récit, not as the composer directs, on the "Jeux de fonds 8 p., Hautbois, Trompette."

On his recordings Tournemire observes Franck's dynamic markings little more than he does the original registrations. When the Hautbois is used as a solo stop the swell box is usually left open—otherwise the solo melody would disappear behind the accompaniment. (Marchal and Duruflé have referred to this phenomenon: see Chapter V.) In the *Cantabile* Tournemire does not close the swell box until m. 24. On the other hand, in the *Pastorale*, since both hands play on the Hautbois of the Récit much of the time, he makes more use of the swell boxes. Generally, however, instead of a smooth crescendo or diminuendo, the swell box jerks open or closed. That a steady crescendo could be accomplished is demonstrated in the course of m. 41–44, even though it is not indicated in the score.

Tournemire is fond of sforzando effects. During the Quasi allegretto of the *Pastorale* he adds sforzandos, immediately followed by subito pianissimos, in passages similar to the following:

Pastorale, m. 69–70

We mentioned previously that in the *Third Choral* Tournemire seldom has the Récit coupled to the Positif, hence, many of the indicated "swellings" are impossible. In the same piece we miss dynamic shadings during the exposition of the choral (m. 30–47). Only a few times in the course of the Adagio of the *Third Choral* are any dynamic marks observed.

Although Tournemire has numerous tempo changes not mentioned in his book, he is faithful to the metronomic markings he gives. The following listing of tempi in the recorded works are followed in parenthesis by the metronome markings published in *César Franck.*

Tournemire begins the *Pastorale* at ♩. = 50 (♩ = 58). However, the passages played on the Positif are taken slower, ♩ = 44. The Quasi allegretto is played at ♩ = 120 (♩ = 100); the fugue (m. 81) ♩ = 100 ("not so fast"). At the a Tempo (m. 98) the tempo returns to ♩ = 120. At the return of the Andantino (m. 147) the tempo, ♩ = 48, is maintained up through m. 159. From m. 167 the tempo fluctuates between ♩ = 46 and ♩ = 52.

The *Cantabile* is played ♩ = 76 (♩ = 69). The tempo is relaxed slightly by m. 65 and from there until the end of the piece ♩ = 72 is maintained.

The opening tempo of the *Third Choral* is ♩ = 112 (♩ = 100). At the exposition of the choral (m. 30) Tournemire slows down to ♩. = 92 although he says in his book the original tempo, i.e., ♩ = 100, should be maintained. The Adadio (m. 96) is played ♪ = 80 (♪ = 76). The third and last side of the *Third Choral* begins at the second beat of m. 117. Here the tempo is ♩ = 88. By m. 143 it has increased to ♩ = 108. An accelerando begins m. 128 and another at m. 144 which continues until the second half of the third beat of m. 145. *Le double plus vite (Movt. du commencement)* is played between ♩ = 116 and 120. By m. 173 the tempo is still ♩ = 116.

Tournemire's playing is devoid of the studied, polished elegance we have come to associate with the performers of his generation. He plays with neither a mannered subjectivity nor a literal objectivity. Rather he performs in a clean, legato style. The tempi are always controlled, although not necessarily slow or conservative, and close to those which he indicated in *César Franck*.

In Tournemire's recorded performances we can identify several of the factors which contribute to the "freedom and imagination" advocated in his book on Franck. The first is rhythmic subtlety: his beat is always flexible rather than distorted; his disciplined rubato never destroys the basic pulse. Another is variation in the interpretation of similar passages: if a passage is repeated, different notes will be stressed. Rhythmic agogic accent is used rather than articulation: prolongation of non-chord tones, emphasis of melodic elements, a stretching of motivic devices. His playing further displays a frequent disregard for and addition of dynamic markings, ritardandi, accelerandi and fermate. He generally uses the solo reed stops alone, rather than in combination with other stops indicated by Franck. Whether this is done for better fidelity on the recording or a general habit, we cannot say. He is not adverse to changing the composer's registration completely, as at the end of the *Pastorale* and *Cantabile*.

SUMMARY

❧ ❧

After examining the contemporary source material, we can conclude that César Franck was a musician whose integrity in composition, performance and teaching was widely admired not only by his
students but by his fellow musicians. That he extended this serious-
ness of approach to all phases of the organ was considered the utmost
in musical dedication at a time when the king of instruments sat
shakily on its throne.

Throughout his career as organist, Franck placed great emphasis on
form in composition and exactitude in execution. Maintaining these
high standards eventually brought him to the most prestigious organ
position in France—professor of organ at the Conservatoire National
—and insured many performances of his organ works during his
lifetime.

As a young organ student at the Conservatoire, Franck excelled in
structuring very formal improvisations. He later applied this composi-
tional logic to his written organ compositions, molding them in
classical forms and imbuing them with ingenious counterpoint.

Franck was served in his organ works by the homogeneity of the
Cavaillé-Coll organs available to him throughout his career. That
builder pursued a style whose tonal and mechanical properties provided Franck with the impetus to compose his works. That he published no works until he could create them at Sainte-Clotilde is significant. And, that the sounds and mechanical appliances of that instrument shaped the forms of his works is irrefutable.

This unique union of instrument and music is most immediately handed down to us by the writings and recordings of Charles Tourne-mire. His detailed performance instructions coupled with the actuality of his recordings at Sainte-Clotilde provide an inestimable milestone on the path toward an authentic interpretation of the organ works of César Franck.

Examples of Plainchant Harmonized in Four-part Counterpoint

from

Charles Tournemire, *Précis d'exécution, de registration et
d'improvisation à l'orgue* (Paris: Max Eschig, 1936) 105.

Example 1. Cantus firmus in the bass.

Example 2. Cantus firmus in the soprano.

APPENDIX B

Examination Pieces Played by the Students
in César Franck's Organ Class June 1874 to June 1890

ᕦᗩᕤ

J. S. Bach: Fugue in G minor, BWV 578
Fugue in C minor (Legrenzi), BWV 574
Concerto in A minor (Vivaldi), BWV 593
Fugue in C minor, BWV 537
Pastorale, BWV 590
Fugue in G minor, BWV 131a
Fugue in D minor, BWV 539 or
Toccata in D minor (Dorian), BWV 538
Prelude in E♭, BWV 552
Fantasie in C minor, BWV 537
Fugue in F minor (Well-Tempered Clavier I),
  BWV 857
Fugue in D minor (Well-Tempered Clavier II),
  BWV 875
Fugue in D minor, BWV 565
Prelude and Fugue in A minor, BWV 543
Prelude and Fugue in E minor, BWV 555
Fantasie in G minor, BWV 542
Fugue in G minor, BWV 542
Fugue in D major, BWV 532
Sonata in C minor, Movement I, BWV 526
Prelude in G major, BWV 541
Prelude in G major, BWV 568
Passacaglia, BMV 582
Aria (Couperin), BMV 587

César Franck: Pièce en Ut [Fantaisie, Op. 16]
Prière, Op. 20

G. F. Handel: Concerto in B♭

Felix Mendelssohn: Sonata No. 3 in A major

SOURCE

Marcelle Benoit, "César Franck et ses élèves," *L'Orgue*, No. 83
(April-Sept. 1957) 76-78.

107

Specification of the Organs Played by César Franck

I. Conservatoire National de Musique

Builder Unknown   Compass: Manuals, 54 notes: „C - '''F
In use from c. 1810.   Pedal, 20 notes: „C - ,G

GRAND-ORGUE
8 Montre
8 Bourdon
8 Flûte (?)
4 Prestant

RÉCIT
5 "expressive" free-reed stops.

108

PÉDALE

16 Bourdon
8 Flûte

and some "expressive" free-reed stops.

SOURCE

Norbert Dufourcq, "L'Enseignement de l'orgue au Conservatoire National avant la nomination de César Franck (1872)," *L'Orgue*, No. 144 (Oct.–Dec. 1972) 123.

II. Église de Notre-Dame-de-Lorette

Cavaillé-Coll Organ   *1839*
Inaugurated: 22 October ~~1883~~

Compass: Grand-Orgue 54 notes:,,C - '''F
          Positif
          Récit, 37 notes: ,F - '''F
          Pédale, 21 notes: ,,,A - ,F
          Flûte, 18 notes: ,,C - ,F
          Reeds, 21 notes: ,,,A - ,F

II. GRAND-ORGUE

16 Montre
16 Bourdon (,C)
8 Montre
8 Bourdon
8 Dessus de flûte conique ('C)
4 Prestant
4 Flûte douce
3 Nasard
2 Quarte de nasard
1 $\frac{3}{5}$ Tierce
V Cornet
III Grand Fourniture
III-IV Petite Fourniture
IV Cymbale
8/16 Bombarde (,,C - ,C: 8', ,C - ''F: 16')
8 Trompette
8 Dessus de hautbois (,F)
4 Clairon

I. POSITIF

8 Montre
8 Bourdon
8 Salicional
4 Prestant
4 Flûte
2 $\frac{2}{3}$ Nasard
2 Doublette
1 $\frac{3}{5}$ Tierce
IV Fourniture
III Cymbale
8 Trompette
8 Cromorne
4 Clairon

PÉDALE		III. RÉCIT EXPRESSIF	
16	Flûte ouverte	8	Bourdon
8	Flûte ouverte	8	Flûte traversière
4	Flûte ouverte	4	Flûte
16	Bombarde	4	Flûte octaviante
8	Trompette	2	Flageolet
4	Clairon	III	Cornet
		16	Cor anglais
		8	Trompette
		8	Hautbois
		8	Voix humaine

Note: When the roman numeral is placed before the name of the division, in a specification, it indicates the position of that division's manual in the console—I being the bottom manual and ascending in order.

PÉDALES DE COMBINAISON

Tirasse Grand-Orgue
Anches Grand-Orgue
Positif au Grand-Orgue
Récit au Grand-Orgue
Expression Récit

SOURCE

Georges Lhôte, "Remarks on the French Organ," *ISO-Information*, No. 1 (Feb. 1969) 72. This specification has been compared with the names of the stops which "... can still be seen on the chests."

Roland Galtier and Kurt Lueders, "L'Orgue Cavaillé-Coll (1838) de l'église Notre-Dame-de-Lorette à Paris et sa 'Restauration,'" *La Flûte Harmonique*, IX (1979) 15.

Note: Félix Raugel's article ("Les Orgues de Notre-Dame-de-Lorette de Paris," *L'Orgue*, No. 111, July-Sept. 1964, p. 84) quotes the specifications of the organ proposed in 1833, not the organ actually built in 1838.

III. Église de Saint-Jean-Saint-François

Cavaillé-Coll Organ
Inaugurated: 29 December 1846

Compass: Grand-Orgue, 54 notes:
„C - ʼʼʼF
Récit, 37 notes: ,F - ʼʼʼF
Pedal, 20 notes: „C - ,G

GRAND-ORGUE	RÉCIT	PÉDALE
8 Montre	8 Flûte harmonique	16 Flûte ouverte
8 Bourdon	8 Voix céleste ✳	16 Bombarde
8 Salicional	4 Flûte octaviante	
4 Prestant	2 Octavin	
2⅔ Nasard	8 Trompette	
2 Doublette	8 Cromorne	
III Plein jeu	8 Cor anglais	
8 Trompette		
4 Clairon		

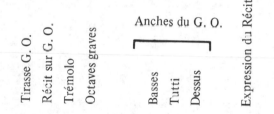

✳ The Récit probably didn't have a Voix cl. The organ was delivered 24 Dec. 1845 & the Viole de Gambe was probably among the 7 stops mentioned by Huybens. The organ was rebuilt around 1861 at which time the V.C. may have been added.

PÉDALES DE COMBINAISON

Tirasse G. O.
Récit sur G. O.
Trémolo
Octaves graves
Anches du G. O.
Basses
Tutti
Dessus
Expression du Récit

SOURCES

Félix Raugel, *Les Grandes Orgues des Églises de Paris* (Paris: Fischbacher, 1927) 181-82.

Georges Schmitt, "Nouveau Manuel complet de l'Organiste," *Encyclopédie Roret* (Paris, 1855). Quoted in François Sabatier, *La Palette sonore de Cavaillé-Coll.* (Paris: Revue "Jeunesse et Orgue," 1979).

Saint-Jean-Saint-François, Organ Case

Kurt Lueders

IV. Église de Saint-Eustache

Ducroquet Organ
Inaugurated: 26 May 1854

Compass: Manuals, 54 notes: „C - ‴F
            Pedal, 30 notes: „C - ’F

PÉDALE	I. GRAND-ORGUE	IV. BOMBARDE
32 Flûte	16 Montre	16 Bourdon
16 Flûte	8 Montre	16 Gambe
16 Bourdon	8 Flûte harmonique	8 Gambe
16 Contrebasse	8 Flûte à pavillon	8 Bourdon
8 Flûte	8 Bourdon	8 Salicional
8 Deuxième flûte	4 Prestant	8 Quintadène*[1]
8 Salicional*	4 Flûte ouverte	4 Salicional*
8 Violoncelle*	2 $\frac{2}{3}$ Nasard	16 Bombarde*
4 Flûte*	2 Doublette	8 Trompette*
4 Salicional*	IV Cymbale	4 Clairon*
32 Bombarde*	V Cornet	
16 Bombarde*	V Fourniture*	
16 Basson*	16 Euphone*	
8 Première trompette*	8 Première trompette*	
8 Deuxième trompette*	8 Deuxième trompette*	
8 Basson*	4 Clairon*	
4 Clairon*		
4 Basson*		

II. POSITIF	III. RÉCIT
8 Montre	16 Bourdon
8 Flûte harmonique	8 Flûte harmonique
8 Bourdon	8 Flûte ouverte[3]
8 Kéraulophon	4 Flûte octaviante
4 Salicional[2]	16 Trompette
4 Flûte harmonique	8 Trompette*
V Plein jeu	8 Euphone*
16 Cor anglais*	8 Trompette-hautbois
8 Trompette*	8 Voix humaine
8 Basse de basson (30 notes)	4 Clairon*
8 Hautbois (37 notes)	
8 Hautbois (free-reed, 37 notes)	
8 Cromorne*	
4 Clairon*	

---

[1] Abbé H.-J. Ply, *La facture moderne étudiée a l'orgue de Saint-Eustache* (Lyon: Perrin et Marinet, 1878) 165, lists this as a 4′ Quintadène.

[2] *ibid.*, 318, 8′ Voix céleste.

[3] *ibid.*, 319, 8′ Bourdon.

Cathedral of Luçon, Organ Console

(Originally intended for the Cathedral of Carcassonne)

SOURCE

Abbé H.-J. Ply, *La facture moderne etudiée à l'orgue de Saint-Eustache* (Lyon: Perrin et Marinet, 1878) 164-66.

* An asterisk appears in the specification to identify stops which are controlled by the Anches ventil of the division.

V. Cathédrale de Carcassonne

Cavaillé-Coll Organ
Played by Franck at the builder's
factory on 30 August 1856.

Compass: Manuals, 54 notes: ,,C - '''F
          Pedal, 27 notes: ,,C - 'D

I. POSITIF	II. GRAND-ORGUE	III. GRAND-RÉCIT EXPRESSIF
8 Montre	16 Montre	16 Quintaton
8 Bourdon	16 Bourdon	8 Bourdon
8 Salicional	8 Montre	8 Flûte harmonique
4 Prestant	8 Bourdon	8 Salicional
4 Flûte douce	8 Flûte harmonique	8 Gambe
3 Quinte	8 Viole de gambe	4 Dulciane
2 Doublette	4 Prestant	16 Bombarde*
8 Trompette	4 Viole d'amour	8 Trompette*
8 Cromorne	4 Flûte octaviante*	8 Hautbois*
4 Clairon	3 Quinte*	8 Voix humaine*
	2 Doublette*	4 Clairon*
	IV Fourniture*	
	III Cymbale*	
	16 Bombarde*	
	8 Trompette*	
	4 Clairon*	

IV. PETIT-RÉCIT EXPRESSIF	PÉDALE
8 Flûte douce	16 Contrebasse
8 Flûte harmonique	8 Basse
8 Viole d'amour	4 Octave
4 Flûte octaviante	16 Bombarde*
2 Octavin	8 Trompette*
8 Trompette harmonique*	4 Clairon*
8 Basson-hautbois*	
8 Voix humaine*	

PÉDALES DE COMBINAISON

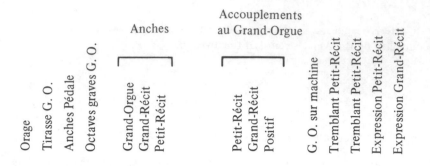

In 1861 this organ was installed in the Cathedral of Luçon.[1]   At that time the third clavier, Grand-Récit expressif, was returned to its original, pre-1856 state—a single free-reed manual, called *Euphone*. The present specification has been reconstructed from two sources. The first is "contracts in the archives of Aude, giving details of the instrument before the addition of the Grand-Récit."[2] The second source is César Franck's manuscript of the first version of the *Fantaisie in C* in which the composer identifed most of the Pédales de Combinaison by number and listed most of the stops of the Grand-Récit in the registration at the beginning of the piece.

SOURCES

Jesse Eschbach and Robert Bates, "Preface," *César Franck: Fantaisie für die Orgel in Drei Versionen* (Bonn-Bad Godesberg: Forberg, 1980).

Abbé Delhommeau, *Orgues et Organistes de la Cathédrale de Luçon,* (Luçon, 1966) 16-18.

---

[1] Delhommeau, *Orgues et Organistes de la Cathédrale de Luçon,* 16-18.
[2] Eschbach, "Preface."

VI. Église de Sainte-Clotilde

Cavaillé-Coll Organ   Compass: Manuals, 54 notes: „C - ‴F
Inaugurated: 19 December 1859   Pedal, 27 notes: „C - ’D

I. GRAND-ORGUE

16 Montre
16 Bourdon
8 Montre
8 Flûte harmonique
8 Gambe
4 Prestant
4 Octave*
3 Quinte*
2 Doublette*
  Plein jeu*
16 Bombarde*
8 Trompette*
4 Clairon*

II. POSITIF

16 Bourdon
8 Montre
8 Bourdon
8 Flûte harmonique
8 Gambe
8 Salicional
4 Prestant
4 Flûte octavinate*
3 Quinte*
2 Doublette*
  Plein jeu harmonique*
8 Trompette*
8 Cromorne*
4 Clairon*

III. RÉCIT

8 Flûte harmonique
8 Bourdon
8 Viole de gambe
8 Voix céleste
4 Flûte octaviante*
2 Octavin*
8 Trompette harmonique*
8 Basson-hautbois
8 Voix humaine
4 Clairon*

IV. PÉDALE

32 Quintaton
16 Contrebasse
8 Flûte
4 Octave
16 Bombarde*
16 Basson*
8 Trompette*
4 Clairon*

PÉDALES DE COMBINAISON

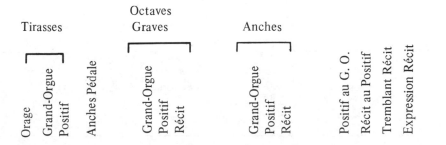

Tirasses
  Orage
  Grand-Orgue
  Positif

Octaves Graves
  Anches Pédale
  Grand-Orgue
  Positif
  Récit

Anches
  Grand-Orgue
  Positif
  Récit

  Positif au G. O.
  Récit au Positif
  Tremblant Récit
  Expression Récit

SOURCE

The preceding is a complete specification drawn from the Sources cited below. For a detailed analysis, see Chapter V.

Joseph Bonnet, "Preface," *Three Chorals of César Franck,* July-Sept. 1942 (New York: J. Fischer, 1948) 3.

Félix Raugel, *Les Grandes Orgues de Paris,* p. 205-06.

Albert Schweitzer, *Deutsche und französische Orgelbaukunst und Orgelkunst* (Leipzig: Breitkopf & Härtel, 1906) 49.

Disposition of the Drawknobs on the Console
of the Organ of Sainte-Clotilde

The preceding composite specification has been distributed according to the photographs of the original console.

Left Stop Jamb

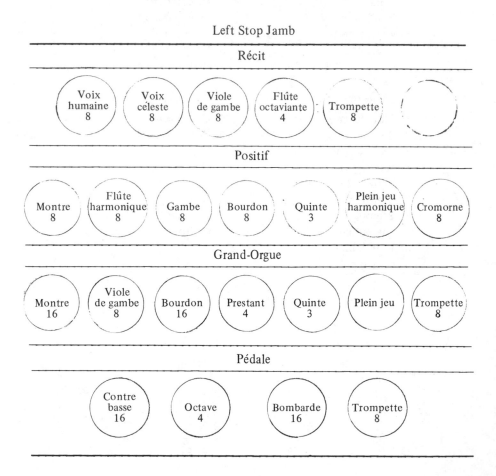

Récit

Voix humaine 8 — Voix céleste 8 — Viole de gambe 8 — Flûte octaviante 4 — Trompette 8

Positif

Montre 8 — Flûte harmonique 8 — Gambe 8 — Bourdon 8 — Quinte 3 — Plein jeu harmonique — Cromorne 8

Grand-Orgue

Montre 16 — Viole de gambe 8 — Bourdon 16 — Prestant 4 — Quinte 3 — Plein jeu — Trompette 8

Pédale

Contre basse 16 — Octave 4 — Bombarde 16 — Trompette 8

Right Stop Jamb

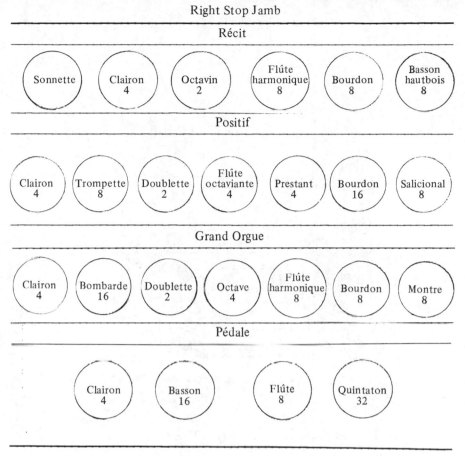

Récit

Sonnette	Clairon 4	Octavin 2	Flûte harmonique 8	Bourdon 8	Basson hautbois 8

Positif

Clairon 4	Trompette 8	Doublette 2	Flûte octaviante 4	Prestant 4	Bourdon 16	Salicional 8

Grand Orgue

Clairon 4	Bombarde 16	Doublette 2	Octave 4	Flûte harmonique 8	Bourdon 8	Montre 8

Pédale

Clairon 4	Basson 16	Flûte 8	Quintaton 32

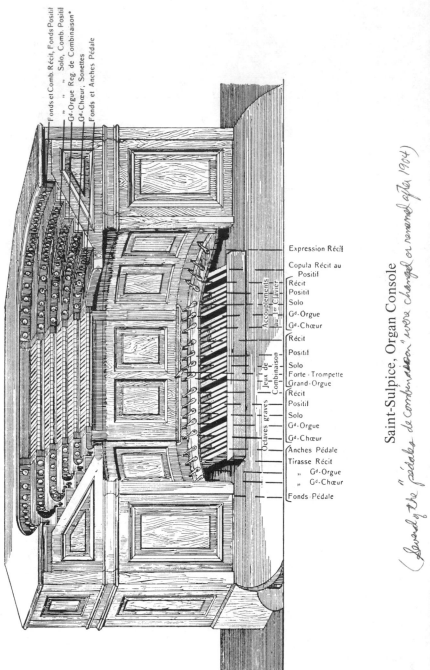

Fonds et Comb. Récit, Fonds Positif
" " Solo, Comb. Positif
" Gd-Orgue Reg. de Combinaison*
Gd-Chœur, Sonettes
Fonds et Anches Pédale

Expression Récit

Copula Récit au
 Positif

Accouplements au 1er Clavier {
Récit
Positif
Solo
Gd-Orgue
Gd-Chœur

Jeux de Combinaison {
Récit
Positif
Solo
Forte - Trompette
Grand-Orgue

Octaves graves {
Récit
Positif
Solo
Gd-Orgue
Gd-Chœur

Anches Pédale
Tirasse Récit
 " Gd-Orgue
 " Gd-Chœur

Fonds - Pédale

Saint-Sulpice, Organ Console

(several of the pédales de combinaison were changed or renamed after 1904)

VII. Église de Saint-Sulpice

Cavaillé-Coll Organ
Inaugurated: 20 April 1862

Compass: Manuals, 56 notes: „ C - '"G
Pedal, 30 notes: „C - 'F

I. GRAND-CHOEUR

8	Salicional
4	Octave
IV	Grosse Fourniture
VI	Grosse Cymbale
IV	Plein jeu
V	Cornet
16	Bombarde
16	Basson
8	1re Trompette
8	2e Trompette
8	Basson
4	Clairon
2	Clairon-Doublette

II. GRAND-ORGUE

16	Principal harmonique
16	Montre
16	Bourdon
16	Flûte conique
8	Montre
8	Diapason
8	Bourdon
8	Flûte harmonique
8	Flûte traversière
8	Flûte à pavillon
5$\frac{1}{3}$	Grosse quinte
4	Prestant
2	Doublette

III. BOMBARDE

16	Sousbasse
16	Flûte conique
8	Principal
8	Bourdon
8	Flûte harmonique
8	Gambe
8	Violoncelle
8	Kéraulophone
5$\frac{1}{3}$	Grosse quinte*
4	Prestant
4	Flûte octaviante
4	Octave*
3$\frac{1}{5}$	Grosse tierce*
2$\frac{2}{3}$	Quinte*
2	Octavin*
V	Cornet*
16	Bombarde*
8	Trompette*
8	Baryton*
4	Clairon*

IV. POSITIF

16	Violon-Basse
16	Quintaton
8	Flûte traversière
8	Quintaton
8	Salicional
8	Viole de gambe
8	Unda maris
4	Flûte octaviante
4	Dulciana
2$\frac{2}{3}$	Quinte*
2	Doublette*
1$\frac{3}{5}$	Tierce*
1$\frac{1}{3}$	Larigot*
1	Piccolo*
I-VI	Plein jeu harmonique*
16	Euphone*
8	Trompette*
8	Clarinette*
4	Clairon*

V. RÉCIT

16	Quintator
8	Flûte harmonique
8	Bourdon
8	Violoncelle
8	Voix céleste
4	Prestant
4	Flûte octaviante
4	Dulciana*
2	Doublette
2	Octavin*
IV	Fourniture*
V	Cymbale*
V	Cornet*
16	Bombarde*
16	Cor anglais
8	Trompette harmonique*
8	Trompette*
8	Basson-hautbois
8	Cromorne
8	Voix humaine
4	Clairon*

PÉDALE

32	Principal-Basse
16	Contre-Basse
16	Sousbasse
8	Flûte
8	Violoncelle
4	Flûte
32	Contre-Bombarde*
16	Bombarde*
16	Basson*
8	Trompette*
8	Ophicléide*
4	Clairon*

PÉDALES DE COMBINAISON

Tirasses	Octaves Graves	Jeux de Combinaison	Accouplements au Grand-Choeur

Orage | Grand-Choeur, Grand-Orgue | Anches Pédale | Grand-Choeur, Grand-Orgue, Bombarde, Positif, Récit | Grand-Orgue, Bombarde, Positif, Récit | Grand-Choeur, Grand-Orgue, Bombarde, Positif, Récit | Tremblant du Récit | Expression du Récit

SOURCE

Abbé Pierre Henri Lamazou, *Étude sur l'orgue monumental de Saint-Sulpice et la facture d'orgue moderne* (Paris: Repos, [1863]) 23-26.

VIII. Église de Saint-Étienne-du-Mont

Cavaillé-Coll Organ
Inaugurated: 26 April 1863

Compass: Positif, 52 notes: „C - '''D
           Grand Orgue, 54 notes: ,C - '''F
           Récit,   42 notes: ,C - '''F
           Pédale, 27 notes: „C - 'D

I. POSITIF		II. GRAND-ORGUE	
8	Montre	16	Montre
8	Dessus de flûte	16	Bourdon
8	Bourdon	8	Montre
4	Prestant	8	Dessus de flûte (harmonique)
$2\frac{2}{3}$	Nasard	8	Bourdon
2	Doublette	8	Gambe
$1\frac{3}{5}$	Tierce	4	Prestant
IiI	Fourniture	4	Octave
III	Cymbale	2	Doublette
8	Trompette	III-IV	Plein jeu
8	Cromorne	V	Cornet
4	Clairon	16	Bombarde
		8	Trompette
		4	Clairon

III. RÉCIT EXPRESSIF

8 Bourdon
8 Salicional
8 Voix céleste
4 Flûte octaviante
2 Octavin
8 Trompette
8 Hautbois
8 Voix humaine

PÉDALE

16 Sousbasse
 8 Flûte
16 Bombarde
 8 Trompette
 4 Clairon

PÉDALES DE COMBINAISON*

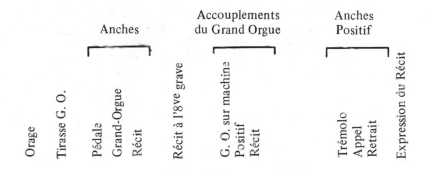

*In 1911 the bottom of the Récit was extended and five of the pédales de combinaisons were added. (Raugel, *Les Grandes Orgues de Paris,* 25-26.)

SOURCE

Félix Raugel, "Du Second au Troisième Grand Orgue de St-Étienne-du-Mont," *L'Orgue,* No. 90 (April-June 1959) 43.

IX. Église de Saint-Denis-du-Saint-Sacrement

Cavaillé-Coll Organ
Inaugurated: 10 October 1867

Compass: Manuals, 54 notes: „C - "'F
Pedal, 25 notes: „C - 'C

I. GRAND-ORGUE

16	Montre
8	Montre
8	Bourdon
8	Viole de gambe
4	Prestant
4	Dulciana (conique)
V	Cornet
16	Bombarde
8	Trompette
4	Clairon

II. POSITIF

8	Flûte
8	Bourdon
8	Voix céleste
4	Prestant
4	Dulciana
2	Doublette
III	Plein jeu
8	Trompette
8	Cromorne

III. RÉCIT

8	Flûte harmonique
8	Viole de gambe
4	Flûte
2	Octavin
8	Trompette
8	Hautbois
8	Voix humaine

PÉDALE

8	Sous-Basse
8	Flûte
8	Violoncelle
4	Octave
16	Bombarde
8	Trompette

PÉDALES DE COMBINAISON

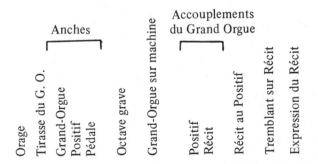

SOURCE

Raugel, *Les Grandes Orgues de Paris,* 176. This was a rebuild of the 1839 Daublaine & Callinet organ whose Gambes, Clarinette and Basson were praised by Berlioz and Meyerbeer more for their orchestral tone than their "organic" character.

X. Cathédrale de Notre-Dame-de-Paris

Cavaillé-Coll Organ   Compass: Manuals, 56 notes: „C - "'G
Inaugurated: 6 March 1868   Pedal, 30 notes: „C - 'F

I. GRAND CHOEUR

8	Principal
8	Bourdon
4	Prestant
$2\frac{2}{3}$	Quinte
2	Doublette
$1\frac{3}{5}$	Tierce
$1\frac{1}{3}$	Larigot
$1\frac{1}{7}$	Septième
1	Piccolo
16	Tuba magna*
8	Trompette*
4	Clairon*

II. GRAND-ORGUE

16	Violonbasse
16	Bourdon
8	Montre
8	Flûte harmonique
8	Viole de gambe
8	Bourdon
4	Prestant
4	Octave*
2	Doublette*
II-V	Fourniture*
II-V	Cymbale harmonique*
16	Basson*
8	Basson*
4	Clairon*

III. BOMBARDE

16	Principal-basse
16	Sous-basse
8	Principal
8	Flûte harmonique
$5\frac{1}{3}$	Grosse quinte
4	Octave
$3\frac{1}{5}$	Grosse tierce
$2\frac{2}{3}$	Quinte*
$2\frac{2}{7}$	Septième*
2	Doublette*
II-V	Grand Cornet*
16	Bombarde*
8	Trompette*
4	Clairon*

IV. POSITIF

16	Bourdon
16	Montre
8	Flûte harmonique
8	Bourdon
8	Salicional
8	Unda maris
4	Prestant
4	Flûte douce*
2	Doublette*
1	Piccolo*
III-VI	Plein jeu harmonique*
16	Clarinette basse*
8	Cromorne*
4	Clarinette aiguë*

V. RÉCIT

16	Quintaton
8	Flûte traversière*
8	Quintaton
8	Viole de gambe
8	Voix céleste
4	Flûte octaviante*
4	Dulciana
$2\frac{2}{3}$	Quinte*
2	Octavin*
II-V	Cornet harmonique*
16	Bombarde*
8	Trompette*
16	Basson-hautbois
8	Clarinette
8	Voix humaine
4	Clairon*

PÉDALE

32	Principal-basse
16	Contrebasse
16	Sousbasse
$10\frac{2}{3}$	Grosse quinte
8	Flûte
8	Violoncelle
$6\frac{2}{3}$	Grosse tierce
$5\frac{1}{3}$	Quinte*
$4\frac{4}{7}$	Septième*
4	Flûte
32	Contre Bombarde*
16	Bombarde*
16	Basson*
8	Trompette*
8	Basson*
4	Clairon*

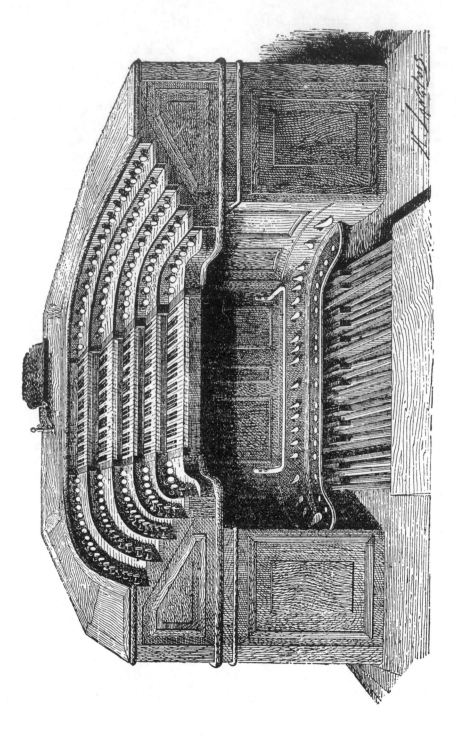

Notre-Dame-de-Paris, Organ Console

PÉDALES DE COMBINAISON

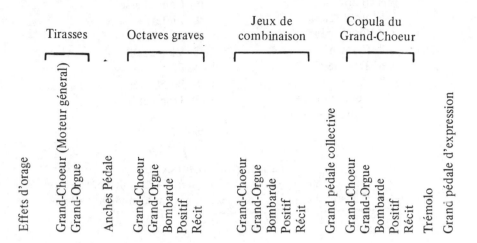

| | Tirasses | | | Octaves graves | | | | Jeux de combinaison | | | | Copula du Grand-Choeur | | | | | | |

Effets d'orage · Grand-Choeur (Moteur géneral) · Grand-Orgue · Anches Pédale · Grand-Choeur · Grand-Orgue · Bombarde · Positif · Récit · Grand-Choeur · Grand-Orgue · Bombarde · Positif · Récit · Grand pédale collective · Grand-Choeur · Grand-Orgue · Bombarde · Positif · Récit · Trémolo · Grand pédale d'expression

SOURCE

François Sabatier, *Les aventures du grand orgue de Notre-Dame-de-Paris au XIXe siècle, II/1859-1963* (Paris: L'Orgue, 1975) 56-62.

XI. Église de La Trinité

Cavaillé-Coll Organ
Inaugurated: 16 March 1869

Compass: Manuals, 56 notes: „C - ’’’G
Pedal: 30 notes: „C - ’F

I. GRAND-ORGUE	II. POSITIF
16 Montre	16 Quintaton
16 Bourdon	8 Flûte harmonique
8 Montre	8 Salicional
8 Bourdon	8 Unda maris
8 Flûte harmonique	4 Prestant
8 Gambe	4 Flûte octaviante
4 Prestant	⅄ 2 Doublette
* 2 ⅔ Quinte	⅄ 1 Piccolo
⅄ V Plein jeu	* V Cornet
⅄ V Cornet	⅄ 16 Basson
⅄ 16 Bombarde	⅄ 8 Trompette
⅄ 8 Trompette	⅄ 8 Clarinette
⅄ 4 Clairon	*8* *Principal*
+4 (Flûte) douce	*4 (Flûte) douce*

III. RÉCIT

- 8 *Gambe*
- 8 (Flûte) *Traverse*
- 8 Bourdon
- 8 Voix céleste
- * 4 (Flûte) *octaviante*
- * 2 Octavin
- * 8 Trompette
- 8 Hautbois
- 8 Voix humaine
- * 4 Clairon

PÉDALE

- 32 Bourdon
- 16 Contrebasse
- 8 Flûte
- 8 ~~Bourdon~~ BASSE
- 8 Violoncelle
- 4 ~~Flûte~~ *Octave*
- * 16 Bombarde
- * 8 Trompette
- * 4 Clairon
- 16 *Sousbasse*
- O *Tacet*
- O *Sonnette (bellows signal)*

PÉDALES DE COMBINAISON

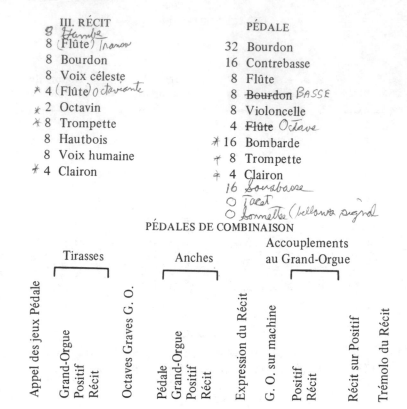

Tirasses   Anches   Accouplements au Grand-Orgue

Appel des jeux Pédale — Grand-Orgue — Positif — Récit — Octaves Graves G. O. — Pédale — Grand-Orgue — Positif — Récit — Expression du Récit — G. O. sur machine — Positif — Récit — Récit sur Positif — Trémolo du Récit

SOURCE

Raugel, *Les Grandes Orgues de Paris,* 219-20.

XII. Conservatoire National de Musique
1871-1908

Compass: Manuals, 54 notes: ,,C - '''F
                 Pedal, 25 notes: ,,C - 'C

GRAND-ORGUE

- 8 Dessus de montre
- 8 Flûte
- 8 Bourdon
- 4 Prestant
- 8 Trompette

RÉCIT

- 8 Flûte
- 8 Gambe
- 8 Voix céleste
- 4 Flûte
- 8 Hautbois (free reeds)
- 8 Trompette

PÉDALE

16 Sousbasse
8 Flûte
4 Flûte
8 Basson

When the Château des Tuileries burned in 1871 the remains of the organ in the chapel was used to build a new teaching instrument for the Conservatoire.[1] Vierne described this organ in his memoirs:

The entire organ was enclosed in an expression chamber. The volume was controlled by a foot lever provided with two notches. There were two manual-to-pedal couplers, a swell to great coupler, a reversible piston for the great Trompette, the same for the swell Trompette and for the pedal Basson. The Montre and the Prestant were impossible to use . . . .[2]

SOURCE

Norbert Dufourcq, *Autour des Orgues de Conservatoire National et de la Chapelle des Tuileries* (Paris: Floury, 1952) 26.

XII. Le Palais du Trocadéro
La Salle des Fêtes

Cavaillé-Coll Organ
Inaugurated: Alexandre Guilmant,
7 August 1878. Played by
César Franck, 1 October 1878.

Compass: Manuals, 56 notes: „C - ’"G
Pedal, 30 notes: „C - ’F

I. GRAND-ORGUE	III. RÉCIT	II. POSITIF
16 Montre	16 Quintaton	16 Bourdon
16 Bourdon	8 Flûte harmonique	8 Principal
8 Montre	8 Cor-de-nuit	8 Flûte harmonique
8 Flûte harmonique	8 Viole de gambe	8 Salicional
8 Bourdon	8 Voix céleste	8 Unda maris
8 Violoncelle	4 Flûte octaviante	4 Flûte octaviante
4 Prestant	2⅔ Quinte	2⅔ Quinte*
4 Flûte douce	2 Octavin*	2 Doublette
V Dessus de Cornet*	16 Basson*	16 Basson*
V Plein jeu harmonique*	8 Trompette*	8 Trompette*
16 Bombarde*	8 Basson-hautbois	8 Cromorne* ·
8 Trompette*	8 Voix humaine	*III-IV Plein jeu*
4 Clairon*	4 Clairon harmonique*	
2 Doublette	*V Cornet*	
	I-III Carillon	

[1] Louis Vierne, *Mes Souvenirs* (Paris: Les Amis de l'Orgue, 1970) 22.
[2] *ibid.*

PARIS. — LE PONT D'IÉNA ET LE¹ TROCADÉRO.

Le Palais du Trocadéro

PÉDALE

32 Principal basse
16 Contrebasse
16 Sous-basse
16 Grosse flûte
16 Violon basse
 8 Grosse flûte
 8 Basse
 8 Bourdon
 8 Violoncelle
32 Contre-bombarde
16 Bombarde
16 Basson
 8 Trompette
 8 Basson
 4 Clairon
 4 Baryton

IV. SOLO

16 Bourdon
 8 Diapason
 8 Flûte harmonique
 8 Violoncelle
 4 Flûte octaviante
 2 Octavin
16 Tuba magna*
 8 Trompette harmonique*
 8 Clarinette*
 4 Clairon harmonique*

PÉDALES DE COMBINAISON

Tirasses				Anches					G. O. sur machine	Accouplements de Grand-Orgue			Récit sur Positif	Octaves Graves				Trémolo			
Orage	Grand-Orgue	Positif	Récit	Pédale	Grand-Orgue	Positif	Récit	Solo		Positif	Récit	Solo		Grand-Orgue	Positif	Récit	Solo	Positif	Récit	Expression Positif	Expression Récit

SOURCES

Jean Huré, *L'Esthétique de l'Orgue* (Paris: Senart, 1923) 87-90.
Wallace Goodrich, *The Organ in France* (Boston: The Boston Music Company, 1917) 124.

Le Palais du Trocadéro, La Salle des Fêtes

Jim Lewis

XIV. Église de Saint-Merry

Clicquot Organ
Rebuilt by Cavaillé-Coll, 1857
Rebuilt by Cavaillé-Coll, 1878
Inaugurated: 29 October 1878

Compass: Manuals, 54 notes: „C - '"F
            Pedal,   27 notes: „C - 'D

I. GRAND-ORGUE

16	Montre
16	Bourdon
8	Montre
8	Dessus de flûte
8	Dessus de gambe
4	Prestant
4	Dulciane
2	Doublette
IV	Fourniture
III	Cymbale
V	Cornet
16	Bombarde
8	Trompette
4	Clairon

PÉDALE

16	Flûte
8	Flûte
16	Bombarde
8	Trompette
4	Clairon

II. POSITIF

8	Montre
8	Bourdon
8	Dessus de flûte
2 $\frac{2}{3}$	Nasard
2	Doublette
1 $\frac{3}{5}$	Tierce
V	Plain jeu
8	Trompette
8	Basson-hautbois
8	Cromorne

III. RÉCIT

8	Flûte harmonique
8	Bourdon
4	Flûte octaviante
4	Viole
2	Octavin
8	Trompette
8	Dessus de hautbois
8	Voix humaine

PÉDALES DE COMBINAISON

Anches   Accouplements   Positif
              au Grand-Orgue

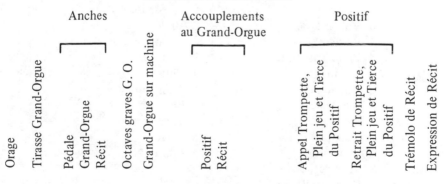

Orage Tirasse Grand-Orgue Pédale Grand-Orgue Récit Octaves graves G. O. Grand-Orgue sur machine Positif Récit Appel Trompette, Plein jeu et Tierce du Positif Retrait Trompette, Plein jeu et Tierce du Positif Trémolo de Récit Expression de Récit

SOURCE

Norbert Dufourcq, *Le Grande Orgue et Les Organistes de Saint-Merry de Paris* (Paris: Floury, 1947) 33-34.

XV. Église de Saint-François-Xavier

Fermis et Persil Organ
Inaugurated: 29 February 1879

Compass: Manuals: 61 notes: „C - ″″C
Pedal: 30 notes: „C - 'F

I. POSITIF

16 Bourdon
8 Bourdon
8 Flûte douce
8 Flûte harmonique
8 Gambe
8 Unda maris
4 Prestant*
4 Salicional
2 $\frac{2}{3}$ Quinte*
2 Doublette*
Plein jeu*
16 Basson*
8 Trompette*
8 Hautbois basson*
4 Clairon*
Sonnette
Cloches

II. GRAND-ORGUE

16 Montre
16 Bourdon
8 Montre
8 Bourdon
8 Flûte harmonique
8 Quintaton couvert
8 Salicional
8 Gambe
8 Octave*
4 Salicional
4 Tierce* (sic) 3 $\frac{1}{5}$?
2 $\frac{2}{3}$ Quinte*
2 Doublette
Plein jeu*
Cornet*
16 Bombarde*
8 Trompette*
4 Clairon*

III. RÉCIT

16 Bourdon
8 Bourdon
8 Flûte harmonique
8 Dulciana
8 Gambe
8 Voix céleste
4 Prestant*
4 Flûte octaviante
2 $\frac{2}{3}$ Quinte*
2 Doublette*
2 Octavin
1 Piccolo
Plein jeu*
16 Bombarde*
8 Trompette*
8 Hautbois basson*
8 Clarinette*
8 Voix humaine*
4 Clairon*

PÉDALE

32 Grand Quintaton ouvert
16 Grande flûte
16 Contrebasse
16 Sous-basse
8 Grosse flûte
8 Viole
6 $\frac{2}{5}$ Octave quinte (sic)
8 Bourdon
4 Flûte
16 Bombarde*
16 Basson*
8 Trompette*
8 Basson*
4 Clairon*

PÉDALES DE COMBINAISON

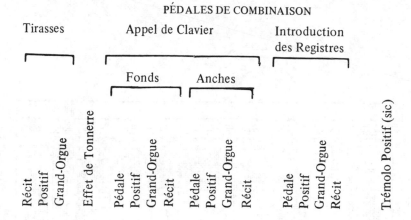

Tirasses

Appel de Clavier

Introduction
des Registres

Fonds   Anches

Récit
Positif
Grand-Orgue

Effet de Tonnerre

Pédale
Positif
Grand-Orgue
Récit

Pédale
Positif
Grand-Orgue
Récit

Pédale
Positif
Grand-Orgue
Récit

Trémolo Positif (sic)

PÉDALES

d'Accouplement

de Renversements
de Clavier

de Transposition
Grave

Positif à Grand-Orgue
Récit

Positif Anches à Récit Anches
Positif Fonds à Récit Fonds
Récit Fonds à Positif Fonds
Récit Anches à Positif Anches

Pédale Anches
Positif Fonds
Grand-Orgue Fonds
Récit Fonds

Effet de Crescendo

BOUTONS D'INTRODUCTION DES REGISTRES

Pédale Anches
Positif Anches
Grand-Orgue Anches
Récit Anches
Trémolo Récit

SOURCE

(Fermis et Persil), *Orgue Monumental de Saint-François-Xavier* (Paris: 1879).

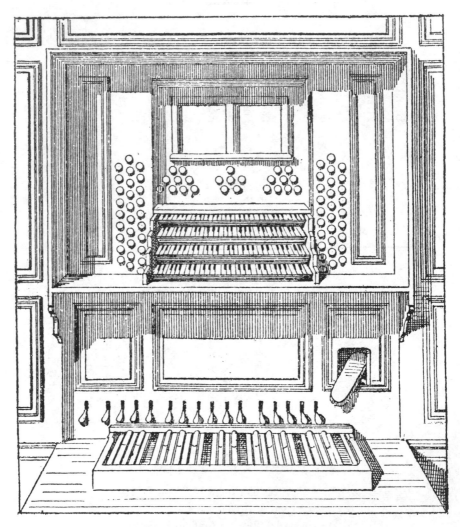

Saint-Eustache, Merkin Organ Console

XVI. Église de Saint-Eustache

Merklin Organ
Inaugurated: 21 March 1879

Compass: Manuals: 54 notes: „C - '"F
Pedal: 30 notes: „C - 'F

I. GRAND-ORGUE	II. POSITIF	III. RÉCIT
16 Montre	16 Bourdon	16 Bourdon
8 Montre	8 Montre	8 Principal
8 Flûte harmonique	8 Flûte harmonique	8 Flûte harmonique
8 Bourdon	8 Bourdon	8 Bourdon (s)
8 Gemshorn	8 Kéraulophon	8 Viole de gambe (s)
8 Viole de gambe	4 Fugara	8 Voix céleste (s)
8 Flûte à pavillon	4 Flûte harmonique	4 Prestant
4 Prestant	2 Doublette	4 Flûte octaviante
4 Rohrflûte	1 Jeu de clochettes	2 Flageolett (sic)
2 ⅔ Nazard	Plein jeu*	1 Piccolo (s)
2 Doublette	16 Clarinette*	8 Cornet*
Fourniture et Cymbale*	8 Trompette*	16 Trombone*
III-VI Cornet*	8 Cromorne*	8 Trompette harmonique*
8 Trompette*	4 Clairon*	8 Basson-hautbois (s)
8 Clarinette*		8 Voix humaine (s)
4 Clairon*		4 Clairon*

IV. BOMBARDE	PÉDALE
16 Bourdon	32 Principal
16 Gambe	16 Flûte
8 Gambe	16 Sousbasse
8 Salicional	16 Contrebasse
8 Quintaton	10 ⅔ Quinte ouverte
4 Dulciana	8 Grosse-flûte
16 Cornet*	8 Bourdon
16 Bombarde*	8 Violoncelle
8 Trompette*	4 Flûte
8 Cor anglais*	32 Bombarde*
4 Clairon*	16 Bombarde*
	16 Basson*
	8 Trompette
	8 Basson*
	4 Clairon*

PÉDALES DE COMBINAISON

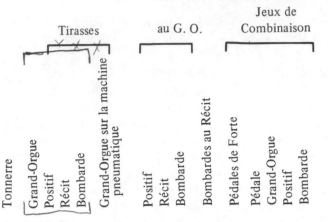

The stops of the Récit were divided into three groups above the top manual. Each group had its own Trémolo and its own ventil with which it could be brought on or off. The unmarked stops in the Récit division comprised the "Jeu de fond," those marked (s) "Jeu de solo," and those marked with the asterisk (*), "Jeu de combinaisons."

SOURCE

Ply, *La facture moderne etudiée à l'orgue de Saint-Eustache*, 238, 241-43.

XVII. Église de Saint-Jacques-du-Haut-Pas

Merklin Organ
Inaugurated: 27 ~~June~~ *May* 1889

Compass: Manuals, 56 notes: ,,C - '''G
Pedal, 30 notes: ,,C - 'F

ORGUE DE TRIBUNE	ORGUE DE CHOEUR
GRAND-ORGUE	GRAND-ORGUE EXPRESSIF
16 Bourdon	16 Bourdon
8 Montre	
8 Flûte harmonique	8 Flûte harmonique
8 Bourdon	
8 Salicional	8 Salicional
4 Prestant	
	4 Flûte octaviante
	4 Dulciane
V Cornet (from old organ)	
16 Bombarde	
8 Trompette	8 Trompette
4 Clairon	4 Clairon

RÉCIT EXPRESSIF

8 Flûte traversière
8 Rohrflûte
8 Viole
8 Voix céleste
4 Flûte octaviante
2 Octavin
IV Fourniture progressive
8 Trompette harmonique

RÉCIT EXPRESSIF

8 Montre
8 Bourdon
8 Gambe
8 Unda maris
4 Prestant
2 Doublette

8 Basson-hautbois
8 Voix humaine

PÉDALE

16 Flûte
8 Violoncelle
4 Flûte
16 Bombarde
8 Trompette
4 Clairon

PÉDALE

Tirasse from each clavier
only

SOURCE

Pierre Hardouin, "Le grand orgue de Saint-Jacques-du-Haut-Pas," *Connaissance de l'orgue* No. 4 (1972) 25.

Published Accounts of César Franck's Organ Performances

꧁꧂

Contents

I. INAUGURATION OF THE GRAND ORGAN OF THE CHURCH OF SAINT-EUSTACHE

Finally the day had arrived when one of the most beautiful and most musical churches of Paris was going to take possession of its grand organ, the former one having been destroyed by flames ten years ago! It was last Friday that, in the presence of an immense crowd, the solemnity took place and that the work undertaken by the celebrated builder, M. Ducroquet, revealed its excellence. The Association of musicians took charge of organizing the ceremony, ordering the program, and conducting the performance. In this circumstance the Association again proved itself worthy of the task; each of the invited eminent guests performed in turn and nobly competed for *la palme du talent*.

M. Lemmens, first organist to H. M. the King of Belgium, had made the journey from Brussels to Paris; it was he who first occupied the stage, to which he returned two more times; M. Cavallo, organist of Saint-Vincent-de-Paul; M. Bazille, organist of Saint-Élizabeth, and M. Franck, organist of Saint-Jean-Saint-François, performed in turn. Under their talented hands, the magnificent instrument successively displayed all its riches and we admired its pure sonority, the variety of sounds made truly remarkable by the differences of timbres. We have already said that the organ, built by M. Ducroquet, has four manuals of 54 notes.

M. Lemmens first played an *Introduction and Fugue* of his own composition on the *Laudate Dominum,* his own *Prière in E*, and the *Final* of Mendelssohn's *First Sonata*. Later he played an *Offertoire in G,* a *Prière in C*, and a *Fugue in C minor*; and finally, a *Prelude and Fugue in E minor* of Bach, a *Prière in F*, followed by an improvisation. In this broad and profound part, M. Lemmens conveyed to us the great qualities which we have already recognized in him when he came to play the organ of Saint-Vincent-de-Paul. He distinguishes himself among his rivals particularly by the strength and the unaffectedness of style. Above all he wants to be a classicist; he is a direct descendent of Bach and refuses the least concession to popular or modern taste which he feels is not in keeping with the dignity of the instrument.

M. Cavallo, whose reputation is well established, distinguished himself in two improvisations, the first of which seemed a masterpiece of conception, structure, ensemble, and details. If it had been absolutely necessary to award the prize of the day, we would have given it, without hesitation, to this perfect piece, regretting that it could not have been recorded by a musical stenographer.

M. Bazille also twice improvised with a youthful facility—a little frivolous, perhaps, for the vaults of a Christian temple.

M. Franck energetically performed a fantaisie composed with care.

Singing had its place between all these pieces. A choir of adults and children under the direction of M. Hurard, maître-de-chapelle of Saint-Eustache, sang a *Sancta Maria* by Cherubini, a psalm of Roeder, a *Laudate* by Adolphe Adam, and the *Domine salvum*. Battaille and Mlle. Caroline Duprez sang a *Veni sancte Spiritus* accompanied by harps, composed by the soprano's father. Mlle. Duprez sang another piece as a solo, *Pastoris aeterni*, by the same composer, with an accompaniment by the bass clarinet, and Battaille sang the *Pro peccatis* from Rossini's *Stabat Mater*. One can honestly say that the two pieces composed by Duprez, our celebrated singer, have elegant and graceful melodies. His charming daughter sang them with her excellent style and pure angelic voice. If one had not heard Battaille at the theater, one might believe that he only sang in church; indeed, it was in church that he started his brilliant career and developed his rare talent before entering the Conservatoire.

M. l'abbé Gaudreau, the curé of Saint-Eustache, and M. l'abbé Deguerry, his predecessor, mingled holy words with the manifestations of religious art. Under their fecund influence the collection was very productive; the presence of the patronesses sufficed to bring the total figure of the receipts to over 7,000 fr.

Let us not forget that M. Édouard Batiste, professor at the Conservatoire and organist of Saint-Nicolas-des-Champs played the orgue d'accompagnement, and that MM. Prumier, father and son, played the harp accompaniment, and M. B. Duprez, the bass clarinet in the two pieces of which the other Duprez, his brother, is the composer.

SOURCE

P.S., "Inauguration du grand orgue de l'église de Saint-Eustache," *Revue et Gazette musicale de Paris* (21 May 1854) 174–75.

II. DEMONSTRATION OF THE ORGAN BUILT FOR THE CATHEDRAL OF CARCASSONNE

M. Cavaillé-Coll, before delivering the beautiful organ for the Cathedral to the Bishop of Carcassonne, wanted this admirable instrument demonstrated one more time for its numerous admirers. The inter-preter, M. César Franck, an excellent organist, highlighted all the riches and harmonic resources, first by a knowledgeable execution of "severe" music, very well written by himself, and then by brilliant improvisations.

SOURCE

Henry Blanchard, "Auditions musicales," *Revue et Gazette musicale de Paris* (30 August 1856) 247–48.

III. INAUGURATION OF THE ORGAN OF SAINTE-CLOTILDE

The inauguration of the great instrument built for the new church of Sainte-Clotilde by M. Aristide Cavaillé-Coll took place December 19th. Many people had braved the excessive cold and the heavy fog which at that time might have given Parisians and visitors the impression that they were in a completely different country. This audience, in which numerous well-known artists were seen, did not regret the fact that they had accepted M. Cavaillé-Coll's invitation. I shall speak of the organ in another article where I shall treat certain rather serious pertinent questions; today, I will confine myself to a review of the inaugural recital.

M. Franck, âiné, organist of the parish, began with a piece of his own written in a broad and forceful style which made a deep impression on his hearers who also appreciated M. Franck when he turned from his own compositions to draw on those conceived by the genius of Sebastian Bach. It is always a great risk to play the pieces of this composer in public, and, in a certain sense, organists are right when they choose to play their own music rather than Bach's. In my opinion, the difficulty is not so much in materially representing Bach's ideas without making a mistake; it is rather, in being able to exploit all these immense harmonic riches in such a manner as to express all they can produce. When playing Bach's music in public, the artist should first become aware of the fact that in this complicated harmony there is more than notes, more than fingering difficulties, more than awkward sections and other difficulties which can be mastered by practice. Besides this precision, this regularity which is already so difficult to attain, it is necessary to find a way to give color and character to the composition. In a word, one must express the *soul* of this great music; it is only then that it can be interesting, even moving.

One may ask how to find this color, how to express it on the organ, an inexpressive instrument? How? That is the secret of great organists and they are no more capable than I of revealing it to you; because with them, it is intuitive knowledge. They can recognize it but they cannot explain it either to themselves or to others. This seems to have been the aim of M. Franck, and the manner in which he performed the *Fugue in E minor* proved that it was not a vain attempt. Serious studies such as these reveal in him a perserverance and give him, at present, a place among organists of the first order. He showed himself at his best when, resuming his rôle as composer, he played his *Final* on the full organ. In this *Final* one recognized the conception and execution of a true master.

What can be said now of Lefébure-Wély? What can we say of the charming improvisations of the most amiable of organists, of this true representative of our French school? While hearing him, should not our school think about reviving itself and finding as Lefébure did, these elegant forms, these graceful ideas, these pleasant combinations, this piquant use of certain effects, this perfect knowledge of the instrument which makes one immediately feel which stops are appropriate for which theme, and how, with the multitude of details, one achieves a marvelous ensemble.

One recognized the qualities of his admirable talent in the first two improvisations where he was able to demonstrate all the resources of the instrument, presenting, one after another, its different aspects. One heard separately the most interesting stops, the timbres of which seduced the ears.

But the piece in which he excelled and which ravished his hearers was the symphonic improvisation in which, recalling the season of the year we are approaching, he seemed to look for themes in the Christmas gospel, trying to make a scenic tableau of the circumstances which accompanied the birth of Jesus. In this great piece he introduced the rather modern, but very interesting, melody of the hymn *Adeste fideles*, which, played on the Voix humaine and with all the means of expression imagined by the builder, produced the sweetest sensation.

Finally, he closed with a work for full organ on the tune of a well-known carol, *Il est né le divin enfant*. One never wearies of hearing these old French airs, justly admired for their pure and naïve character. Under the skillful and learned hands of our excellent Lefébure, those works of which I speak acquired a new charm at each moment.

I said under his skillful and *learned* hands; he has found people so foolish as to reproach him for exactly that which makes his talent valuable and gives it its essential characteristic, that is, the graceful turn of his thoughts, the sometimes light harmony which he likes to use, and finally, his habit of almost always improvising and never playing written pieces.

And about this last observation and in spite of the irrelevancy of such critics, one cannot believe the simple-minded writers and presume that if M. Lefébure doesn't play written music it is because of a lack of ability, and to believe that he isn't a good enough reader to correctly play the music of the great masters who have gone before.

Furthermore, our improviser recently replied, in the smartest manner, to the partisans of a "learned" music which has such poorly unlearned men as advocates. In *La Maîtrise*, which M. Heugel publishes, M. Lefébure has contributed too few organ pieces in legato style; in these the real science is revaled in its most elegant aspect; in these, perfectly organized and well-developed ideas evolve with the proper use of harmonic richness devoid of all heaviness and enclosed in the limits prescribed by good taste and this sane reason to which the most beautiful imaginations submit themselves without effort, knowing how to combine these easy concessions, emphasize their power and give them priceless advantages.

SOURCE

Adrien de la Fage, "Inauguration de l'orgue de Sainte-Clotilde," *Revue et Gazette musicale de Paris* (5 Jan. 1860) 4.

IV. THE RECEPTION OF THE ORGAN OF SAINT-SULPICE

(Reception, 29 April and the second recital, 2 May)

The organ of Saint-Sulpice, built in 1781 by the celebrated Clicquot and restored in 1845 and 1857, finally attained the highest degree of perfection thanks to the talent of M. Aristide Cavaillé-Coll. The reception of this magnificent instrument drew an enormous crowd of artists and music lovers to Saint-Sulpice last Tuesday, April 29th.

One would have to write a whole volume if one wanted to give an exact idea of all the marvels of this organ—the only one of its kind in the entire world. Because, at this time, we are not able to devote ourselves to this work which is of interest to the history of the organist's art, we will speak today of the reception of the masterpiece and of the talented artists who have made it so famous.

His Eminence Msgr. the Cardinal-Archbishop of Paris presided over the religious ceremony. After the blessing of the organ, the choir of the parish, directed by M. Renard, maître-de-chapelle, performed a religious piece, and between each instrumental performance, the same choir, assisted in the solo parts by Michot, the tenor with an expressive voice, was heard in new sacred choruses, which avoided the monotony which would have resulted from hearing only the organ.

MM. Schmidt, organiste titulaire of the parish; Bazille of Saint-Élizabeth; Franck, aîne, of Sainte-Clotilde; Saint-Saëns of La Madeleine, and also Alexandre Guilmant of Saint-Nicolas of Boulogne-sur-Mer were heard successively. Through an excess of modesty M. Schmidt remained in the background; but, in spite of this, the dignity of his style was noticed. M. Bazille, endowed with a charming imagination, played a pastorale with very successful organ effects. M. Franck was severe without pedantry, and M. Saint-Saëns, profound without obscurity. M. Alexandre Guilmant demonstrated, in a *Méditation* of his own composition, that he was able to unite, without effort, the expressive style with the most elevated science. In conclusion, the success of the reception, after that of the organbuilder, was shared by MM. Bazille and Guilmant.

The following Friday, the talented organist of Boulogne gave a very interesting solo recital. He played successively a *Concerto* of Handel, a *Toccata and Fugue in D minor* of Sebastian Bach, a *Pastorale* of Kullak, and several pieces of his own compostition, among which was a remarkable *Communion* of exquisite sentiment. Finally, the young[1] artist, a student of his father and of the celebrated Lemmens, played a *Marche* in a grand style, arranged by himself, on a theme of Handel.

The organ of Cavaillé-Coll is so complicated that when combining the innumerable stops of which it is composed, it takes more than a month's work to become familiar with it. Alexandre Guilmant hardly had two hours practice! Everyone admired the intelligence of the organist of Saint-Nicolas; and after the recital, the invited artists complimented him enthusiastically. It is good for a young artist to leave his loved ones and his cherished works, to come to Paris hoping to establish his reputation and Alexandre Guilmant, upon his return to Boulogne, will receive congratulations from his family and friends for the glorious excursion which he just made to Paris.

SOURCE

Antoine Elwart, *Revue et Gazette musicale de Paris* (11 May 1862) 155–56.

---

[1] Guilmant was 25 years old.

V.   INAUGURATION OF THE GRAND ORGAN
OF SAINT-ÉTIENNE-DU-MONT

The inauguration of the grand organ of Saint-Étienne-du-Mont, re-built and enriched with notable improvements by the firm of A. Cavaillé-Coll, took place Monday evening, the 26th of last month be-fore a large number of persons, among whom one noticed several artists and distinguished music lovers. Several organists from our principal parishes demonstrated in succession this beautiful instrument which stands behind the richest Louis XIII-style façade and which possesses a great sonority and some stops of a truly remarkable timbre.

M. Franck, aîné, of Sainte-Clotilde, made masterly use of the 16' and 8' foundation stops. M. Auguste Durand, of Saint-Roch, elegantly set off the gambes and the Voix humaine. M. Lebel, organiste of Saint-Étienne-du-Mont, and professor of organ at the Institution des Jeunes Aveugles, proved his musical knowledge in two well-developed pieces. But the greatest triumph went to M. J. Ch. Hesse, one of our pianist-composers, whose name has become most popular recently. M. Hesse is an organist *in partibus*, and the church that employs this artist will be the envy of the other temples of the capital.

SOURCE

Revue et Gazette musicale de Paris (3 May 1863) 143.

VI. ORGAN RECITAL AT SAINTE-CLOTILDE

M. César Franck gave a recital at Sainte-Clotilde last Thursday which was attended by a large number of artists and music lovers. Franck's compositions, written by the hand of a master, were played by him. One notices in the first the happiest effect of a choir of Voix humaines; and in the *Grande Pièce symphonique* a most distinguished melody played first on the Clarinet and later repeated on the Voix célestes. At this recital M. Franck showed himself to be as learned a composer as he is a skillful instrumentalist and will have proved one more time that the standards of French organists are being raised day by day, and that the improvements realized in modern organ building, far from impeding musical composition, on the contrary, lend valuable and powerful assistance.

The beautiful organ of Sainte-Clotilde shone no less in this recital than the learned organist.

SOURCE

Revue et Gazette musicale de Paris (20 Nov. 1864) 375.

VII. ORGAN RECITAL AT SAINTE-CLOTILDE

A select audience gathered Friday, April 13th, in the nave of Sainte-Clotilde to hear the talented organist of this parish, M. Franck, aîné. The various compositions played by M. Franck, conceived in a very severe style which, not excluding variety, made marvelous use of the numerous resources of the organ of Sainte-Clotilde, one of Cavaillé-Coll's best instruments. Liszt, in whose honor this recital was given, complimented M. Franck on the elevated style of his works and his magisterial execution.

SOURCE

"Nouvelles," *Revue et Gazette musicale de Paris* (22 April 1866) 126.

VIII. SOLEMN INAUGURATION OF THE ORGAN OF NOTRE-DAME

The solemn inauguration of the new organ of Notre-Dame, built by Aristide Cavaillé-Coll, took place at 8 o'clock, Friday evening, March 6th. Until we speak in detail of the structure of this magnificent instrument, we will say a few words about the ceremony and the performers.

The Cathedral was crowded; one may assume that this crowd, more curious than attentive, somehow disturbed, by its noisy attitude, the imposing effect of the solemnity and that the sonority of the instrument was also impaired. And then, nine organ works, one after the other, including the Introduction and Sortie played by the organiste titulaire, M. Sergent! It was much too long.

MM. Loret of Saint-Louis-d'Antin; Aug. Durand of Saint-Vincent-de-Paul; Chauvet of Saint-Merry; Saint-Saëns of La Madeleine; César Franck of Sainte-Clotilde; Guilmant of Boulogne-sur-Mer; Widor of Lyon were heard successively; all played their own music with the exception of M. Loret who performed a Prelude and Fugue of Bach. Among this avalanche of modern pieces one must mention two of real merit which were acclaimed unanimously; the *Noël* of M. Chauvet and the *Marche* from the Cantata for the Exposition of M. Saint-Saëns.

Some psalms with faux-bourdons, an *Ave Maria*, a *Pater*, and an *Agnus Dei*, performed under the direction of M. Félix Renaud, alternated with the organ. Mgr. Darboy, Archbishop of Paris, blessed the instrument.

SOURCE

"Concerts et auditions musicales de la semaine," *Revue et Gazette musicale de Paris* (18 March 1868) 85.

IX. INAUGURAL RECITAL OF THE GRAND ORGAN
OF LA TRINITÉ

The inaugural recital of the grand organ of La Trinité ought to have opened with the *Offertoire* from the *Messe Solennelle* of Rossini[1] played by the organiste titulaire, M. Chauvet. This piece would have been more striking by comparison as the little organ in use at the Théâtre Italien was powerless to reproduce these sonorities; moreover, the talented artist had carefully prepared it according to the tradition preserved by M. Georges Mathias, who interpreted it for the first time at Comte Pillet-Will's, under the eyes and with the indications of Rossini. Among the very large audience which filled the church, many people had come in the hope of hearing it; but the director of the Théâtre Italien had decided otherwise.

A court order, addressed to M. le Curé of La Trinité, reached the organist; M. Bagier forbade the performance of the *Offertoire* under the pretext of *prejudice grave* against his interests. One looked in vain to discover where this prejudice lay, which, moreover, is subject to a point of law. Therefore, the *Offertoire* was not performed; and, in view of the importance which it had to the recital program, M. Chauvet didn't want to substitute anything for it.

The other organists gathered to take part in this ceremony displaying the numerous resources of the instrument were heard in the following order: M. Henri Fissot of Saint-Merry, played a *Méditation religieuse* of sober effects but great serenity and beautiful character; M. Ch. M. Widor of Lyon, an *Andante* and a *Scherzo* in which he displayed a, very great technical skill; M. Saint-Saëns of La Madeleine, a *Bénédiction nuptiale*, a piece of little effect and few ideas—this does not mean that the composer lacks talent; M. August Durand,[2] a *Fantaisie pastorale* in which there were entirely too many reminiscences; M. César Franck of Sainte-Clotilde, a vigorous well-developed improvisation in

---

[1] Rossini lived in the parish of La Trinité and had been a member of the commission for the new organ (as he had been the previous year for that of Notre-Dame). His funeral was held in La Trinité on 21 November 1869.

The *Petite messe solennelle* was composed in 1864 and the private performance referred to, at the house of the banker Pillet-Will, was given on 14 March 1864. Written for the accompaniment of harmonium and two pianos, Rossini afterwards scored it for full orchestra. In this form it had been publicly performed at the Théâtre-Italien on 28 February 1869, only two weeks before the inauguration of the organ of La Trinité.

[2] Durand founded his famous publishing house this same year—1869—the firm which published all of César Franck's organ music.

which he sought to point up the greatest possible number of sonorities.

Several choruses and solos sung by MM. Bollaert, Marie, Grisy, &c., alternated with the organ. Finally, M. Chauvet ended the ceremony with a brilliant *sortie en forme de marche* which he prefaced with the motif of the *Offertoire*, forbidden the church and monopolized by the Théâtre; an ingenious protest which received general approval.

SOURCE

"Concerts et auditions musicales de la semaine," *Revue et Gazette musicale de Paris* (16 March 1869) 101.

X. SOCIÉTÉ DE CONCERTS DU CONSERVATOIRE
Third Concert

The eminent organist, M. César Franck, was applauded for the severe beauties of a *Prelude and Fugue in E minor* of J.S. Bach. It was quite an accomplishment because the applause seemed sincere.

SOURCE

Ch. Bannelier, *Revue et Gazette musicale de Paris* (5 Jan. 1873) 5.

XI. FOURTEENTH ORGAN RECITAL IN THE SALLE DES FÊTES OF THE PALAIS DU TROCADÉRO

The recital given by M. C. Franck [Tuesday, 1 October 1878 at three o'clock in the afternoon] summed up, so to speak, the man himself: composer, improvisateur and executant, and, with the authority of a master, he proved himself equal to the entire program. Three new and unpublished works of his own composition have been heard for the first time at this recital. The *Fantaisie en la* is a beautiful piece, very skillfully wrought; but all the details were not brought out well— the soft stops lacking presence and distinctness in the hall. The *Cantabile in B major*, an expressive melody of noble character, was more effective thanks to the telling *Récit* stop employed. The *Pièce héroïque*, although containing some excellent things seemed less interesting than the two other works. As for the *Grande Pièce symphonique in F-sharp minor*, it has long been known and justly appreciated; the *andante*, as always, was warmly welcomed. In his program M. Franck had devoted a large part to improvisation for which all real musicians had to be grateful. His free-style treatment of themes of Félicien David (first chorus from *Le Désert*), Berlioz (two motifs from *l'Enfance du Christ*), Bizet (two motifs from *L'Arlésienne*), created charming details. He was particularly successful with Berlioz' themes. At the end he returned again to that interesting part of the organist's art, by improvising on Russian themes (two pretty popular motifs), Swedish, Hungarian and English themes, first treated separately, then superimposed. The motifs were too numerous and it would not have been possible to take advantage of each one sufficiently without fatiguing the audience. With this slight reservation, we are happy to pay homage to the most elevated and the most complete talent we know. We have congratulated ourselves once more that such a peerless artist is at the head of organ teachers in France.

SOURCE

"Nouvelles Musicales de l'Exposition." *Revue et Gazette musicale de Paris* (6 Oct. 1878) 321.

XII. SOLEMN AUDITION OF THE GRAND ORGAN OF SAINT-MERRY

The grand organ of Saint-Merry has just been restored and completely repaired by M. Cavaillé-Coll. A solemn *audition* of this instrument, thus renovated and endowed with important improvements, took place recently. M. Wachs, organiste titulaire, Franck and Gigout played some beautiful pages of Bach, Mendelssohn, Boëly, etc.

SOURCE

"Nouvelles diverses," *Revue et Gazette musicale de Paris* (10 Nov. 1878) 366–67.

XIII. INAUGURATION OF THE GRAND ORGAN OF SAINT-FRANÇOIS-XAVIER

The inauguration of the grand organ constructed for the Church of Saint-François-Xavier by MM. Fermis et Persil, took place Thursday, February 27th. We did not attend this solemnity and it is not entirely our fault because the programs erroneously indicated the date as Thursday, *March* 27th. We are obliged to confine ourselves, then, to a brief description of the success obtained by the instrument—which is very beautiful and powerful (4,406 pipes, one 32' stop, fourteen 16' stops, ten mutation stops, fournitures, etc.)—and render a short verdict of the talent of the composers and performers (MM. Franck, Widor, Gigout and Albert Renaud, the organiste titulaire) who brought out the qualities of the instrument and who played several of their works.

M. Faure sang Niedermeyer's *Pater noster* magnificently; the *Ave verum* of M. A. Renaud, sung by M. Vergnet and accompanied by the violinist, M. Paul Viardot, the choirs and orchestra, produced a great effect. M. Colonne conducted the ensemble performances.

SOURCE

Revue et Gazette musicale de Paris (9 March 1879) 78.

XIV. SOLEMN INAUGURATION OF THE ORGAN OF SAINT-EUSTACHE, 1879

The solemn inauguration of the beautiful organ of Saint-Eustache, restored and enlarged by M. J. Merklin, took place Friday, March 21 in the presence of a large and sympathetic audience. The repairs and additions of the expert builder are considerable and were carried out in all parts of the instrument: claviers, action, reservoirs, windchests, machines, pneumatic motors, stops and voicing. The organ, built by Ducroquet in 1854 and long in disrepair since it was damaged by shells in 1871, is today one of the best and most complete in existence.

Several eminent Parisian artist lent their assistance to the inaugural ceremony. We cite in the first rank M. C.-A. Franck, organist of Sainte-Clotilde and professor of organ at the Conservatoire, who played his beautiful *Fantaisie en la*; designated on the program under the title *Cantabile*, a well-developed piece of great elevation of style, full of rich ideas and new details. This Fantaisie has already been played with great success at the concert given by the composer at the Trocadéro. M. Th. Dubois, organist of La Madeleine, then played some excerpts from his *Paradis perdu*, one of the two scores which won the competition of the City of Paris. Then M. Gigout, organist of Saint-Augustin, played his *Marche funèbre* and his transcription of the *Aria for Pentecost*[1] of Sebastian Bach, and improvised on a plainchant with much facility and great purity of form.

[1] "My heart ever faithful."

After a Dominican priest's address, mostly devoted to musical art, M. Guilmant, organist of La Trinité, played his *Méditation en la*, and magnificently executed the colossal *Toccata in F* of Sebastian Bach; then he improvised for a long time in a very interesting manner, concentrating on putting in relief all the stops of the organ and especially those with which the instrument is newly endowed by M. Merklin; among those, one noticed, the Voix humaine, the Clochette, and a Flûte harmonique in the Pédale whose timbre reminds one of the horn and the violincello at the same time. Finally, the organiste titulaire of Saint-Eustache, M. Dallier, who was awarded first prize at the last concours of the Conservatoire, revealed his solid and brilliant talent in a fantaisie on some themes of his late predessor, Édouard Batiste, and in a symphonic excerpt of which he is the composer.

In conclusion, several pieces had been sung by MM. Lauwers and Lemarche: except for the attractive *Pater noster* of Niedermeyer, it is hardly worthwhile mentioning them except to say that the *Ave verum* and the *Tantum ergo* are arrangements: the first of an aria from *Don Juan*, the second of a love duet from *The Creation* and which, consequently, were ill chosen for a religious ceremony.

SOURCE

Revue et Gazette musicale de Paris (30 March 1879) 101.

CÉSAR FRANCK, ORGAN TEACHER
BY ALBERT MAHAUT*

~~❦~~

I was still a child at the École Nationale des Jeunes Aveugles de Paris where dedicated teachers, devoted to their art, taught us music.

Each year César Franck visited us; he came to preside over our juries. He was interested in all of us and took specific notice of some of us. It is thus that I first knew him. He announced the prizes in his deep voice. Franck's voice! How beautiful it sounded. How it moved us, we blind, so sensitive to inflections of the voice. . . . He advised us and we listened with rapture. He spoke little, in short phrases, but immediately we fathomed the depth of his soul, his grandeur, his strength, and, at the same time, his kindness. Sometimes he sat at the organ and improvised. Those were feast days of which we spoke long afterwards.

Franck loved our school. He wrote for us and dedicated to us one of his works for choir, organ and orchestra, *Psalm 150*—"Praise ye the Lord!" (1883). It was in our chapel that he himself conducted one of the first complete performances of his *Mass in A*, so well-known today. Our choir surpassed itself in his presence and under his inspiring direction. We, therefore, owed our highest aspirations to César Franck.

When he noticed my organ jury it seemed to me as though a beautiful horizon opened before me. Did I feel then that one day I would rank among the interpreters of his works? I dare not affirm it, but I feel most certainly that it was at that time that my artistic conscience was awakened.

SOURCE

*Albert Mahaut, *César Franck, Professeur d'Orgue*. A pamphlet published in March, 1905. Included in the author's *L'Oeuvre d'Orgue de César Franck* (Paris: Chez l'Auteur, 1923) 15–22.

I was seventeen when I left the school and went to England where I spent two years. I had always wanted to return to Franck. Back in Paris, I went to Sainte-Clotilde to hear the Maître. I found him to be wonderful. He recognized me and wanted me to become his pupil. He helped me to perfect my writing of counterpoint and fugue and, in October, 1888, when he decided I was ready, I entered his organ class at the Conservatoire.

It was an unforgettable year; contact with this superior man three times a week contributed to my artistic evolution. He began his class at eight o'clock, usually coming on foot and always on time, whether he had been up late the preceding night (and he was always up late) or whether he had just returned from a trip the same morning.

How short these classes seemed! No one thought about the passing time until the growing noises from the other side of our door threatened the next invasion.

At first he didn't hear. "Maître, it is M. Bourgault-Ducoudray's class —these are the students from the elocution class who want the room," one dared say. With a plaintive exclamation he tore himself away from the unfinished task, then, acquiescing to the rights of others, he slowly said, "Yes, yes, we must leave."

His combined ardor and serenity overcame us and left an indelible imprint upon us. I could hardly foresee his future fame and I was only vaguely aware of the extent of his genius, but from his being a perpetual *Sursum Corda* rose like a radiant flame whose warmth I felt.

The year passed full of work and full of hope. The Maître was remarkably kind toward all of his students. He encouraged me, he liked me to take the initiative and, when he received a visitor of note, he always invited me. "Come tomorrow," he would write, "and bring your 'tools' "—that is what he called my instruments for writing Braille. I went armed with my tools; he himself dictated a piece of plainchant which I accompanied in florid counterpoint. Unable to use my left hand, which was busy reading the Braille text, I replaced it by a double pedal part, and I managed this feat by playing the bass with the left foot, the tenor with the right foot, the two upper parts in the right hand. This practical procedure always aroused a very lively interest. Then I either improvised a fugue or played one of the Maître's great pieces.

When we improvised, Franck was completely involved—as though we were imbued with his spirit. "I like it," he said simply at good passages. "I like it." Often he only said that, but he put it in such various tones of voice that these words were enough for us to understand his thoughts and to inspire our own, to ennoble our conceptions and compel us to go beyond our limitations.

If sometimes he had to quell some disturbances which arose from some thoughtless group, he would turn abruptly and, at the top of his voice (though still deep), shout a brief word, "Behave!" Instantly order was restored and he returned to the theme or the fugue. The jury arrived and I took first prize—to the joy of the Maître.

In October, 1890, for the last time, Franck resumed his classes at the Conservatoire. But he would only make a few appearances: his vacation had not cured him of a fatal injury (a carriage accident). It was at his house on the Boulevard Saint-Michael that I called on him for the last time. He welcomed me with his invariable kindness. Even at this final hour he forgot about himself. "I'm not well, " he said, and again, lower but effortlessly, "I'm not well"; and he spoke no more of himself. He interested himself affectionately in my career: I had just taken over the harmony class at the École Nationale des Jeunes Aveugles. I told him about it.

"Ah!" he said with an expression that I shall never forget—as though giving his blessing to my new endeavor, "you will do very well there." Then he lavished advice upon me, emphasizing and explaining, from his unique point of view, the fundamental points of harmony, that science of which he had penetrated all the mysteries.

Filled with emotion, I left him. A few days later we were informed of his death and, on a sad November day, we accompanied him to Sainte-Clotilde, then to the cemetary at Montrouge. The faithful who formed the cortège felt the great loss. Yet, no one lost hope. We gathered around a tomb, it is true, but this tomb would be glorious—we felt it.

We resumed our work with courage, each in his own sphere, for the sake of him who, unrecognized during his life, would soon be enthusiastically acclaimed.

CÉSAR FRANCK INTIME: A CONVERSATION WITH M. GABRIEL PIERNÉ BY PIERRE DE LAPOMMERAYE

Among César Franck's students there is one whom circumstances have placed in a position to observe over a long period the life and career of the great composer; M. Gabriel Pierné, after having taken lessons from the maître, remained his faithful disciple and friend. He later succeeded him at Sainte Clotilde and became one of his greatest interpreters. It was, therefore, logical to ask M. Gabriel Pierné for some personal reminiscences about the musician who was just fêted in Liège and whom France, his adopted country, is soon going to honor.

I telephoned M. Gabriel Pierné to ask for an appointment and to explain the purpose of my visit.

"Diable!" replied the distant voice of the maître. "I won't have much to tell you! Come anyway! We'll see."

What a charming host M. Gabriel Pierné was, how many things he has seen, how many he has remembered and how well he tells them—simply, but with humor. His smile hides a certain emotion when he recalls his youth and studies.

"You want some personal reminiscences of Franck? But, of course, you won't ask me my opinion of his work."

"No, maître. The devotion you bring to performances of his works is a testimony; better than words, the fervor with which you conduct them constitutes an opinion."

SOURCE

Pierre de Lapommeraye, "César Franck Intime: Une Conversation avec M. Gabriel Pierné," *Le Ménestrel* (1 Dec. 1922) 484–86.

"Very well, I am going to tell you all that I knew of the intimate Franck. Don't expect a story of an exciting life of romantic adventures. The quiet, hardworking and secluded existence of 'Père Franck' is legendary and, for once, the legend conforms to the truth.

"I knew César Franck at the Conservatoire. A student of Marmontel, I had obtained my first prize in piano and was going into Massenet's composition class. Franck knew me only as a piano virtuoso. One day, upon meeting me, he asked if I didn't intend to play the organ as well. Such a question was an honor for me and, happily, I told him yes. That is the beginning of my relationship with Franck, a relationship which later would become as intimate as it could be between a master like him and a young student which I remained for a long time.

"Franck was a model teacher and M. Rabaud had given him a *satisfecit* for his *exactitude*. Always in a hurry, but always on time, some minutes before the appointed hour one would see him arrive, bounding through the back door of the old Conservatoire. His usual dress had the rigidity of a uniform: frock-coat, top-hat and grey trousers held up so high by his suspenders that they always looked too short. He never forgot his umbrella which he carried hooked over his left arm or allowed it to drag negligently—always at his left side.

"He glanced around the waiting room to see if his students were there. Alas! I am ashamed to confess that in my generation the students of the Conservatoire were late—the room was often empty. Franck would go into the room where the organ was and, while waiting, patiently improvise. If he had to wait a little too long, he went to recruit his students from the class next door. Thus, frequently, in Massenet's class, about two-thirty in the afternoon, we would see the door open, César Franck's head appear and a calm voice, resonant and deep, say, 'Isn't there anyone for me?' Those who were finished in Massenet's class rose and went into the next room.

"And since I just spoke about Massenet's class, I am reminded of how these two teachers, so different in talent and temperament, had a common teaching method. When a student took his composition to Massenet, the latter read it, but he didn't say, 'It's bad. Such a chord is badly placed. You should omit eight measures here, and eight others there.' No, he spoke in general terms, indulgently: 'This is not bad, but look, perhaps this would be better.' Then he sat at the piano, corrected your composition, recomposing it before you in such a manner that it was all taken apart and a new work, like you should have written, emerged. Franck did the same: when you improvised at

the organ, instead of stopping you and making a series of detailed observations, he sat beside you on the bench, helped you with a note,
then two, pushing you little by little, gently taking your place, improvising for you and teaching you by his example. And what admirable
examples! In order to give such lessons, you had to be Massenet or
Franck."

"What did the lessons entail?"

"Improvisations of plainchant, improvisations of florid counterpoint, improvisations of fugue, improvisation of a sonata on a free
theme and, at the end, a piece for performance.

"Père Franck had little notebooks of themes which he always carried
with him. Oh, here they are."

And M. Gabriel Pierné takes from a drawer two rectangular notebooks, one bound in black—the other bound in red. The one bound in
black contained fugue themes which Franck had collected at random.
They were subjects by Bach, Handel, Gluck, Léo Delibes— the subjects
on one side, the answers on the other. In the notebook bound in red
were themes from the classics and Franck's original themes. In leafing
through these notebooks, one is struck by the neatness of the writing
and the care with which each theme is copied with its reference.

After a silence rich with memories: "He always carried them with
him in the inside pocket of his frock-coat," continued M. Gabriel
Pierné. "At a lesson, he took them out and chose a theme that we had
to develop in our improvisation.

"Like all great men, he was extremely indulgent, but he was also
very serious and (was this a quality or a fault?) he didn't have a sense
of humor—whereas his neighbor, Massenet, had one. I remember a
very inoffensive prank we played on Massenet. We removed, little by
little, the horsehair stuffing from his armchair so that, although
Massenet saw the level of the seat go down each day, he couldn't
understand it. We wove hairpieces from the hair. When Massenet,
during one of his classes, noticed me wearing this 'wig,' the truth
suddenly occured to him and, as if by reflex, he exclaimed, 'Ah! it is
you, Pierné. Wait 'til I catch you!" But I had hardly run out of the
room when Massenet came after me, and smiling, said, 'Come on. It
was a good joke. Come back in.' With Franck, because of his heart of
gold, I would have gotten back in, also, but certainly not immediately
and not without reproaches."

And, as I smiled, M. Gabriel Pierné said, "I was then sixteen years
old."

"César Franck was organist of Sainte-Clotilde as well. There, as at
the Conservatoire, he was always in a hurry. He arrived for the high

mass a little before nine o'clock—always in his frock-coat, top-hat and with his umbrella. He passed through the sacristy to check the service list for the week—it was indispensable for him to know it in order for him to be able to arrange his lessons.

"One day a sacristan, undoubtedly very well-informed on the state of health of his congregation, said to him, 'You see, Monsieur Franck, this week we have no weddings, but we have prospects of two beautiful burials within a fortnight.' And Père Franck smiled, but not for long, because of his good nature he thought of the grief which the prediction of the naïve sacristan presaged.

"Franck left hastily for the organ where he tore into the *Kyrie.* The visits of his students hardly began until around nine-thirty."

"After the sermon?"

"That wasn't why they were late. It was because of the improvisations which, as you know take place after the sermon: at the Offertory, the Communion and finally, the Sortie. It was there that Franck was truly unique.

"He took a theme from one of these little notebooks or asked one of his assistants to propose one. Then, the theme chosen, he would reflect before improvising. With his right elbow held in his left hand he would tap his forehead with the third finger of his right hand. And from that moment nothing existed for him but the music—and when he translated it to the organ it was something indescribable. The themes were linked logically, with precision and with an unheard-of ease—all taking on the texture of a great work. One never heard anything as beautiful. Will we ever hear it again? It was too beautiful for the requirements of the mass, because Franck, completely engrossed in his composition, didn't follow the parts of the mass and didn't know when to stop.

"The curé of Sainte-Clotilde had first installed a little bell in the blower room. When this little bell rang, it meant: 'Monsieur Franck, by order of the curé, stop!' But M. Franck, absorbed, did not hear the little bell. Then they put in a louder electric bell. That one Le Père Franck heard (he couldn't do otherwise) but then he would exclaim, 'I never have time to return to the correct key.' And, unruffled, he modulated, following the rules, in order to come back to the original key. During this time one saw the good curé of Sainte-Clotilde impatiently eyeing the organ while the celebrant said his prayers slower. When the return to the key went on too long, the good curé of Sainte-Clotilde, after having opened and closed his breviary several times, always hoping to hear the final chord, got up and went himself to the maîtrise to give two or three imperious rings. Then he confirmed his order by sending a chorister up to the organ. But Franck didn't stop.

"When César Franck died, the curé of Sainte-Clotilde, at the funeral services, gave an admirable oration, but, he perhaps thought to himself, 'Those improvisations were magnificent, but they were very long.' Nevertheless, when I succeeded César Franck as organist of Sainte-Clotilde, the first words the curé uttered were, 'Ah! you know Pierné, at the first sound of the bell, you are to stop!' Probably, when Tournemire succeeded me in 1898 or 1889, they gave him the same order. But the ones who listened to the Maître were ravished.

"What more can I say? Franck was industrious. He divided his time between the Conservatoire, Sainte-Clotilde and his lessons which were so numerous that he didn't know how to schedule them. Thus, I took mine at six o'clock in the morning. The concierge was hardly awake, the servants were still asleep, and Mme. Franck came to open the door. All during my lesson Franck took his *café au lait* and was so alert at that early hour that I envied him."

"You don't like to work in the morning?"

"I have always had a horror of it—and see, that has been my luck! As a student, I had my lesson with Franck at six-fifteen in the morning. Likewise, that with Marmontel at five-thirty in the morning. And now that I have earned the right to sleep late, three times a week I have a rehearsal at nine in the morning!

"His lessons took all of his time. He was not able to compose in the winter so that it was during his vacation, generally during the month of August, that he worked. It was upon his return from the country that he played for us his *Quintette*, his *Variations symphoniques*, and his *Sonate*, thereby showing us, with a charming ingenuity, that we, his students, were part of his intellectual family.

"Franck was little played during his lifetime and it was chiefly at the Concerts-Colonne that his works were given for the first time. Not only did he have difficulty being performed but he was hardly able to find publishers. This didn't bother him. He had no false pride, but he knew his worth. Very modest, he, nevertheless, was sure of himself. Thus, he was always sincerely happy with the public's reception of his works. After an icily-received recital we prudently tried to console him. 'The public didn't understand all the beauty of your work,' we said to him. 'But I am very happy,' he replied. 'The public has been very nice—it's fine that way.'

"He was truly a beautiful soul, with an inexhaustible goodness, and a bit of naïveté—completely honest in his artistic life as well as in his family life. They called him 'le père Franck,' and he was, in effect, a true 'papa' to us all and it was as such that we mourned him.

"Now you realize the profound joy we feel when we see the unanimous homage rendered to him. César Franck has been dead only thirty-two years. You see, this time posterity didn't wait too long to reveal itself clairvoyant."

CÉSAR FRANCK'S ORGAN CLASS IN 1889-1890
BY HENRI BUSSER

I entered the organ class of César Franck—that *sanctuaire musicale* at the old Conservatoire in the Faubourg Poissonière—on the first Monday of October, 1889. The organ stood on a platform at the back of the stage in the small hall of the eighteenth century-style rococo theater. An old two-manual instrument with few resources, it had been renovated by Cavaillé-Coll.

The night before I had gone, without any introduction, to present myself to the Maître at his organ at Sainte-Clotilde. After having looked over my recent work in the harmony, fugue and composition *concours* at the École Niedermeyer, César Franck, with the greatest affability, had said, "Young man, you seem very talented. Come to my class at the Conservatoire tomorrow morning and, without doubt, we will make something of you." I was in seventh heaven!

The next day, with a beating heart, I sat at the organ and played a Mendelssohn sonata and a Bach fugue before improvising several measures on a free theme given me by the Maître. "Not bad, not bad," he said, nodding his head. "I think you will be able to enter my class after the January examination."

I later made the acquaintance of my future comrades: Mlle. Marie Prestat, *excellente musicienne*, Charles Tournemire, Henri Libert, Runner, the blind Vierne, and Dupré, whose improvisations, verging on the operatic, brought joy to our good teacher.

SOURCE

Henri Busser, "La Classe d'Orgue de César Franck en 1889–1890," *L'Orgue* No. 102 (April–June 1962) 33–34.

It is true to say that the teaching of technique was rather neglected —notably pedal study. One prepared works of Bach and Handel for the examinations but most of the time was devoted to plainchant (which was treated very freely in florid four-part counterpoint), and to improvisation of fugue and the free theme. When the student found a way, on a single *échappée*, of introducing an unexpected modulation, César Franck would say delightedly, "J'aime, j'aime!" But when a poor blunderer hesitated, losing himself in endless searching, the Maître suddenly getting red in the face, pushed him aside and then, under his fingers, everything became clear—marvelous. It was a veritable enchantment which aroused our enthusiasm. Among us former students were to be found extraordinary improvisers: Vincent d'Indy, Gabriel Pierné, Cesare Galeotti; still others, Debussy, Dukas, and Bachelet, former pupils of Ernest Guiraud's composition class, came to hear this new teaching in which mysticism dissolved into the purest poetry. I don't think I missed one of those admirable classes in the year!

After the January examination (where I had the good fortune to improvise on a ravishing theme by Léo Delibes), I was received as a pupil. But I was hardly brilliant in the improvisation of fugues and my teacher agreed to give me some private lessons at his home in the Boulevard Saint-Michel.

Before leaving, while putting the usual ten francs (which he usually took per lesson) on the mantle, he said, "My young Busser, I know you aren't rich—keep your money." Some time later he took me aside. "It's your turn to do me a favor. My assistant at Sainte-Clotilde, my student, d'Indy, will be absent. Can you replace him for the mass on Pentecost?" I couldn't recover from the surprise and happiness! Thus, counseled by the maître-de-chapelle, Samuel Rousseau, I became my revered teacher's assistant!

Franck was extremely benevolent. I never heard him criticize his colleagues Saint-Saëns or Massenet; and he had a particular deference for our director, Ambroise Thomas, the composer of *Mignon*. Having been present at a Société des Concerts performance of excerpts from *Psyché*, he told us the next day, "What a fine score that is of our director—what imagination and what talent in orchestration!" forgetting that he, himself, had written a masterpiece (unknown at the time) on the same poetic subject of Psyché.

At the beginning of the month of October, 1890, we did not meet our dear Maître at his class. Suffering for several weeks from a painful injury brought about by a simple carriage accident, César Franck passed away peacefully, without any suffering, leaving to his students the memory of an exceptional teacher whose kindness was equal to his marvelous genius.

PERSONALIA

～⟨ʒʒ⟩～

Certain names cited in the text are not to be found in standard reference works. And while others may be found, their relationship with César Franck or the organ is either slighted or not mentioned at all. We include in this appendix brief sketches of some of the more important of Franck's associates.

ALKAN, Charles Valentin (1813–1888)

Alkan won first prize in organ in Benoist's class in 1834. He was one of the examiners on the jury of the Conservatoire when Franck competed for the first prize in 1838. Alkan and Franck were among those present in the tribune when Lemmens played at Saint-Vincent-de-Paul in February, 1852. In the late 1870's he performed on the pedal-piano ". . . a great part of the organ literature—including all the works of Bach."[1]

> He admired Bach above all other composers, and it was his intense love of Bach's organ music that caused him to take up the pédalier in his later life; he felt that the piano-tone of the pédalier was better suited to the "expressiveness" of Bach's organ works than the organ itself and consequently he performed all these works on the pédalier.[2]

Franck called Alkan "The Poet of the Piano." In 1857 Alkan had composed a Symphony (Nos. 4, 5, 6 and 7 of the *Études, Op. 39*) for

---

[1] Bloch, *Alkan*, 2.
[2] *op. cit.*

piano solo. It may deserve to be remarked that Franck composed the first symphony for organ five years later and dedicated it to his friend, Alkan.

BUSSER, Henri (1872–1973)

Busser entered Franck's organ class in 1889 and later won first prize under Widor. He succeeded Gounod as organist of the parish church of Saint-Cloud in 1892 and remained until 1906.[3] For a while he was choirmaster at the Opéra-Comique and from 1902 until 1939 (and again after 1947) he was conductor of the Opéra. He taught composition at the Paris Conservatoire from 1930 to 1948. He died on New Year's Eve, 1973, just 16 days short of his 102nd birthday.

CHAUVET, Charles-Alexis (1837–1871)

Chauvet won first prize for organ in Benoist's class in 1860. He was a fervent defender of the polyphonic tradition and, with Saint-Saëns, was one of the first neo-classic organists of the French school. Nicknamed "le petit père Bach," he played Bach more than any other Parisian organist. He possessed a remarkable facility at improvisation and it was said that he knew how to accommodate the exigencies of modern harmony with a piquant originality while remaining faithful to the severe character of the instrument and the respect due the sanctity of the temple. Disdaining the "flow'ry style," Camille Dupré wrote that "his manner was grave and learned, a little affected sometimes in its ingenious combinations but always noble in the ensemble and of an imposing effect." He held positions at Saint-Thomas-d'Aquin, Saint-Bernard-de-la-Chapelle (1863), Saint-Merry (1866), and La Trinité (1869).

DUBOIS, Théodore (1837–1924)

In 1858, while still a student at the Conservatoire, Dubois was Franck's accompanist (while he himself was maître-de-chapelle) at Sainte-Clotilde. The following year Dubois won the first prize in organ at the Conservatoire. When the Grand-Orgue was completed and Franck assumed his duties as *organiste titulaire*, Dubois remained as maître-de-

[3] Raugel, *Les Grandes Orgues de Paris*, 253.

chapelle. He spent five years in Italy (from 1861 to 1866) but returned to Sainte-Clotilde where he stayed until 1868 when he assumed the same position at La Madeleine. It was at Sainte-Clotilde that he presented, in 1867, for the first time, his oratorio *Les Sept Paroles du Christ*.

An old curé at Sainte-Clotilde compared Dubois and Franck: "Ah! M. Franck was very boring! He always played as though he were dead tired. But M. Dubois—he delighted us!"[4]

EMMANUEL, Maurice (1862–1938)

Emmanuel attended the Paris Conservatoire from 1880 to 1887 but appears not to have been a student of César Franck. He was maître-de-chapelle at Sainte-Clotilde from 1904 to 1907 and then taught music history at the Conservatoire for the next 30 years.

HINTON, John William (1849–1922)

John Hinton studied privately with Franck in Paris in 1867. Educated at Trinity College, Dublin, Hinton received the degrees of M.A. and Mus. D.[5] He was organist of Saint Michael's and All Angels' Church, Woolwich, from 1891 to 1909 and of the Church of the Ascension, Blackheath, from 1909 to 1912. A professor at the Royal College of Organists in London, he is the author of three books on organ construction.

D'INDY, Vincent (1851–1931)

One of Franck's earliest organ students, d'Indy was enrolled in the organ class in 1873 and, after two years, won only First Accessit. While a student he was organist of the Church of Saint-Leu Taverny, near Ermont.[6] He was a director of the Schola Cantorum and, from 1912, professor of the ensemble class at the Conservatoire. His biography of César Franck is the standard reference work on that composer.

---

[4] Cellier et Bachelin, *L'Orgue*, 188.

[5] *Dictionary of Organs and Organists* (London: Mate & Son, 1922) 359.

[6] Hughes Imbert, *Vincent d'Indy*, translated by Makower in *Studies in Music by Various Authors* reprinted from *The Musician*, ed. Robin Gray, 113.

LEFÉBURE-WÉLY, Louis-James-Alfred (1817–1870)

Lefébure-Wély won first prize in organ in Benoist's class in 1835. He was a celebreated virtuoso, remarkable improviser and a composer of light, elegant and successful music. Organist of La Madeleine from 1847 to 1857 and Saint-Sulpice from 1863 until his death, he possessed so exceptional a pedal technique that Alkan dedicated his *Douze études pour les pieds seulement* to him and Franck dedicated his *Final* to him. He shared with Franck the inaugural recital of the organ of Sainte-Clotilde.

LORET, Clément (1833–1909)

Born at Termonde, Loret was educated largely in his native city. At the age of seven he played the Offertoires and Sorties at the parish church in Termonde and a year later was permitted to play the most difficult parts of the service. As a student at the Brussels Conservatoire, he studied with Fétis and Lemmens, gaining the first prize for organ in 1853. In 1857 he was engaged as professor at the École de Musique Religieuse in Paris and afterwards became its director. He held posts in the Parisian churches of Saint-Louis-d'Antin, the Panthéon and Notre-Dame-des-Victoires.

MAHAUT, Albert (1867–1943)

Mahaut had been a student at the Institution Nationale des Jeunes Aveugles and later a laureate of Franck's organ class at the Conservatoire. Vice-President of l'Association Valentin Haüy (the founder of the Institution Nationale des Jeunes Aveugles in 1784) he summarized the human and religious doctrine of César Franck in a highly significant book, *Le Chrétien, Homme d'Action*. He entered Franck's class in October, 1888 and won first prize in June, 1889 with the *Prière*. Franck described him as an "Élève parfait."[7] He was organist of Saint-Pierre-de-Montrouge from 1892 to 1897 and left to succeed Léon Boëllmann at Saint-Vincent-de-Paul where he remained for two years until 1899. He was professor of harmony at the Institution Nationale des Jeunes Aveugles from 1889 until his retirement in 1924. In 1898 he played the complete organ works of Franck at the Trocadéro.

Vierne described him as ". . . a remarkable person with a keen, cultivated intelligence, exceptional gifts as a virtuoso and great facility in

[7] Benoit, "César Franck et ses élèves," 77.

improvisation. . . ."[8] Upon his resignation from Saint-Vincent-de-Paul he devoted ". . . himself exclusively to the artistic and philanthropic mission which he had been carrying on for forty-five years on behalf of his sightless fellows. . . ."[9]

PIERNÉ, Gabriel (1863–1937)

Pierné won first prize in Franck's organ class at the age of nineteen in 1882. On Franck's death in 1890 Pierné succeeded him as organist of Sainte-Clotilde and held the post until 1898 when his interests turned full-time to composing and conducting. Prominent as conductor of the Concerts Colonne, he was also a member of the administrative committee of the Conservatoire. Franck kept a little notebook in which he marked down comments about each pupil after the twice-yearly juries. His notes on Pierné, January 1881, read: "Fine intelligence. Will be a good student and succeed, I hope . . . Charming pupil, a worker. Open and quick mind. He is still too much 'pianist' and not enough 'organist.' "[10] When he finally won the first prize, 12 June 1882, we read, "A gifted and hard-working student such as one rarely finds."[11]

ROPARTZ, (Joseph) Guy (1864–1955)

After admission to the bar Ropartz decided against a legal profession and entered the Conservatoire as a pupil of Dubois and Massenet and later, Franck. He was director of the Conservatoire in Nancy from 1894 to 1919 and then conductor of the municipal orchestra of Strasbourg until 1929. He was a prolific composer and left a small quantity of organ and harmonium music.

SERRES, Louis de (1864–1942)

De Serres was in Franck's class from the fall of 1885 until he left in January of 1888. Franck wrote that although he was a "good student" and "conscientious," by 1887 his "musical studies were still not very advanced"—even though he played Bach's *Prelude and Fugue in A*

---

[8] *op. cit.*

[9] Vierne, *Mes Souvenirs*, 16.

[10] Benoit, *Ibid*, 77.

[11] *op. cit.*

minor for the January examination! "He suffers pains in his hands and arms which often hamper his work.[12] De Serres taught at the Schola Cantorum from 1900 and when it was reorganized as the École César Franck in 1935 he became its director.

TOURNEMIRE, Charles (1870–1939)

Tournemire succeeded Pierné as organist of Sainte-Clotilde and held the post until his death. He was an organ student at the Conservatoire during Franck's last two years but won the first prize in organ in 1891 in Widor's class. Franck commented that he was an "excellent student, very quiet and a worker."[13] He was professor of ensemble playing at the Paris Conservatoire.

VIERNE, Louis (1870–1937)

Although Vierne studied with Franck for the briefest time of any pupils who have left reminiscences, in his *Souvenirs* he has left us the longest account of Franck as a teacher. Vierne was in Franck's class, first as an auditor, from October, 1889, and as a full student of the Conservatoire from January, 1890. Franck had served on the juries at the Institution Nationale des Jeunes Aveugles where Vierne had studied with Adolphe Marty (himself a Franck pupil) and had become interested in the extremely talented boy.[14]

[12] *op. cit.*

[13] Benoit, "César Franck et ses élèves," 78.

[14] Vierne, *Mes Souvenirs*, 20.

ADDITIONS TO THE FRANCK WERKVERZEICHNIS

꘎꘎꘎

William Mohr's book, *Caesar Franck*, published in 1969, contains the first thematic catalogue of the works of César Franck. The following are additions and corrections to this catalogue.

FWV 26 (1-5)

Cinq Pièces pour Harmonium

Pièces pour Harmonium transcrites pour Grand Orgue par Louis Vierne. (Paris: Leduc, 1901)

FWV 28

Fantaisie, Opus 16
Entstehungszeit: Oct. 1863.

Fantaisie für die Orgel in Drei Versionen contains three complete versions of this *Fantaisie* edited by Jesse Eschbach and Robert Bates. (Bonn-Bad Godesburg: Forberg, 1980)

FWV 29

Grande Pièce symphonique, Opus 17.

Autograph manuscript in the Stiftelsen Musikkulturens Framjande Stockholm, Sweden.

173

FWV 38

Choral I (in E major)
Widmung: à Augusta Holmès

First draft, dated 9 août 1890, is in The Morgan Library, New York City.

FWV 39

Choral II (in B minor)
Widmung: à Augusta Holmès

Facsimile of the autograph manuscript, annotated by Emory Fanning published (Middlebury: 1981). This manuscript was among those autographs auctioned by Sotheby Parke-Bernet and Co., London, on 27 November 1980.

FWV 40

Choral III (in A minor)
Widmung: à Augusta Holmès

FWV 48

Symphonie in D minor

Arranged for organ by Herbert M. Kidd (New York: H. W. Gray, 1928)

FWV 52

Interlude Symphonique de Rédemption

Transcrit pour Orgue par Marcel Dupré (Paris: Bornemann, 1972)

FWV 61

Messe à Trois Voix: Panis Angelicus

Another autograph manuscript (4 pages, 35 1/2 x 27 1/2 cm) is in The Library of Congress, Washington, D. C.

Additions

Pièce en mi bémol (1846)

May be found in *Pièces (d'orgue) inédites de César Franck*, resti-
~1ées par Norbert Dufourcq (Paris: Schola Cantorum, 1973)

Petit Offertoire

First appeared in 1885 in a collection entitled *L'Orgue d'Église* edited by Abbés E. Brune and F. Pierre. It now appears in *Les Mattres Parisiens de l'Orgue au 19ème Siècle* edited by Kurt Lueders. (Bonn-Bad Godesberg: Forberg, 1982) 36–37.

"Intermezzo" from *L'Arlésienne* by Georges Bizet

Entre-acte transcribed for organ and piano duet by César Franck. (4 pp., 35 x 26 cm.) In The Clark Memorial Library, University of California, Los Angeles.

BIBLIOGRAPHY

Alkan, Charles-Valentin. *Préludes et Prières,* Choisis et arrangé pour l'orgue par César Franck. (Paris: Costallat, 1889)

American Guild of Organists. *Revised Report on the Standardization of the Console.* (Approved by The Council of the American Guild of Organists, 11 December 1961)

Audsley, George Ashdown. *The Art of Organ Building,* 2 vols. (New York: Dodd, Mead & Co., 1905)

Benoit, Marcelle. "César Franck et ses élèves," *L'Orgue* No. 83 (April–Sept. 1957) 76–78.

de Bertha, A. "Franz Liszt," *Bulletin français de la S. I. M.* (1907) 1160-84.

Bidwell, Marshall. "Organ music in Paris churches," Part V, Ste.-Clotilde, etc., *The American Organist* VI/1 (Jan. 1923) 14–19.

Billingham, Richard. "Improvisation and Form in the Organ Works of César Franck," *Music* XII/4 (April 1978) 47–49.

Bloch, Joseph. *Charles-Valentin Alkan.* (Privately printed, 1941)

Blondel, G. *Rapport sur le grand orgue de tribune et l'orgue de choeur de l'église Saint-Jacques-du-Haut-Pas à Paris.* (Paris, 1908)

Bonnet, Joseph. "Preface," *César Franck's Three Chorals for Organ.* (New York: J. Fischer, 1948) (Note: Preface written in 1942.)

———. "Bonnet shows how a church in France selects an organist," *The Diapason* (Dec. 1942) 7. (Note: Extract of a speech given at a dinner of the Guilmant Organ School Alumni Association, New York City, 19 October 1942.)

Brink, Hans; Paul Peeters. "Het orgel van César Franck in de Ste. Clotilde: 'Continuing story' of prijsvraag voor organisten?" *Het Orgel* (Sept. 1982) 276–89; (Feb. 1983) 34–49.

de Brisay, A. C. D. "Review of Gramophone Records," *The Organ* X/39 (Jan. 1931) 181-82.

Brook, Barry S. "The simplified plaine and easie code system for notating music, a proposal for international adoption," *Fontes Artes Musicae* XII/2-3 (May–Sept. 1965) 156–60.

Busser, Henri. "La classe d'orgue de César Franck en 1889–1890," *L'Orgue* No. 102 (April–June 1962) 33–34.

Cavaillé-Coll, Cécile et Emmanuel. *Aristide Cavaillé-Coll.* (Paris: Fischbacher, 1929)

Cellier, Alexandre; Bachelin, Henri. *L'Orgue.* (Paris: Delagrave, 1933)

Cellier, Alexandre. *L'Orgue Moderne.* (Paris: Delagrave, 1913)

"César Franck and the organ," *Victorian Organ Journal* VII/4 (March 1979) and VII/5 (April 1979).

Cheney, Winslow. "A Lesson in Playing Franck," *The American Organist* XX/8 (Aug. 1937) 263–67. (Note: Subtitled a "Measure-by-measure outline of the technical details involved in attaining an artistic interpretation of *Pièce héroïque*," its interest for readers today lies in its directions for playing Franck on a period American organ.)

Clunn, Harold P. *The Face of Paris.* (London: Spring Books, n. d. [1960]) 136–37.

Coignet, Jean-Louis. Letter to the author. Châteauneuf-de-Bargis: 15 September 1904) 20–22.

de Courcel, R. *La Basilique de Sainte-Clotilde.* (Paris, 1957)

Davies, Laurence. *César Franck and His Circle.* (London: Barrie & Jenkins, 1970)

———. *Franck.* (London: J. M. Dent, 1973)

Delhommeau, Abbé. *Orgues et Organistes de la Cathédrale de Luçon.* (Luçon, 1966)

Dictionary of Organs and Organists. (London: Mate & Son, 1922)

Demuth, Norman. *César Franck.* (New York: Philosophical Library, 1949)

Dommel-Diény, Amy. *L'Analyse harmonique en examples de J.-S. Bach à Debussy, Fascicule 11: César Franck.* (Paris: Éditions A. Dommel-Diény, 1973) (Note: Pages 43–91 contain an extended analysis of the *Trois Chorals.*)

Douglass, Fenner. *Cavaillé-Coll and the Musicians,* 2 vols. (Raleigh: Sunbury, 1980)

Dubois, Théodore. "Discours de M. Théodore Dubois," *Souvenir du 22 octôbre 1904. A César Franck, ses disciples, ses amis, ses admirateurs.* (Paris: Cabasson, 1904) 20–22.

Dufourcq, Norbert. *Autour des orgues du Conservatoire National et de la Chapelle des Tuileries.* (Paris: Floury, 1952)

———. *César Franck.* (Paris: La Colombe, 1949) (Note: Pages 73–81 translated by Raymond Mabry as "The milieu, work and art of César Franck," *The Diapason* (May 1972) 4–5.

———. "L'Enseignement de l'orgue au Conservatoire National avant la nomination de César Franck (1872)," *L'Orgue* No. 144 (Oct.-Dec. 1972) 121–25.

———. *Eugène Gigout.* (Paris: L'Orgue, Cahiers et Mémoires, No. 27, 1982)

———. *Le grand orgue et les organistes de Saint-Merry de Paris.* (Paris: Floury, 947)

————. *La musique d'orgue française de Jehan Titelouze à Jehan Alain.* (Paris: Floury, 1949) (Note: Pages 135-58 translated by Raymond Mabry as "César Franck and the revolution of the religious spirit," *Music* VIII/7 [July 1974] 27-30.)

Duruflé, Maurice. "Mes souvenirs sur Tournemire et Vierne," *L'Orgue* CLXII/2 (April-June 1977) 1-7.

————. "Notice," *Les Trois Chorals de César Franck.* Revision et Annotations de Maurice Duruflé. (Paris: Durand, 1973)

Eddy, Clarence. "Clarence Eddy gives reminiscences of his eventful musical life," *The Diapason* XXIII/5 (April 1932) 14.

————. "Leading organists of France and Italy," *Music* (Dec. 1896) 163-70.

Edwards, C. A. *Organs and Organ Building.* (London: "The Bazaar" Office, 1881)

Ellingford, Herbert F. "On performing some of César Franck's greater organ works," *The Organ* XXXI (Jan. 1929) 152-60. (Note: Ellingford rearranges the "irritating layout and unnatural notational mannerisms" in many passages to avoid "extreme ledger lines" and "innumerable double sharps.")

Emmanuel, Maurice. *César Franck.* (Paris: Henri Laurens, 1930).

————. "Les Orgues de Sainte-Clotilde," *Le Monde Musical*, 45e année, N° 8 et 9 (Sept. 30, 1934) 245-47.

Eschbach, Jesse; Bates, Robert. *César Franck. Fantaisie für die Orgel in drei Versionen.* (Bonn-Bad Godesberg: Forberg, 1980).

Fanning, Emory M. "The 19th Century French Organ of Cavaillé-Coll and the Organ Works of César Franck," Ph.D. dissertation, Boston University, 1964.

Farmer, Archibald. "The Musician's Bookshelf," *The Musical Times* LXXII/1063 (Sept. 1931) 800-01.

————. "Organ Recital Notes," *The Musical Times* LXXVII/1118 (April 1936) 343-44.

(Farnam, Lynnwood). "A chat with Lynnwood Farnam," *The Musical Times* (Aug. 1, 1923) 543-45.

Faucheur, Jérôme. "Le Grand orgue de la cathédrale d'Ajaccio," *L'Orgue* CL/2 (April-June 1974) 50-53.

Fauquet, Joël-Marie. *Catalogue de l'oeuvre de Charles Tournemire.* (Geneva: Editions Minkoff, 1979)

Fellot, Jean. "Chronologie de l'oeuvre de Cavaillé-Coll," *Orgues Historiques* No. 11 (Paris: C. C. P. Harmonie du Monde, 1965) 18-22.

(Fermis et Persil). *Orgue Monumental de Saint-François-Xavier.* (Paris, 1879)

Gallois, Jean. *César Franck.* (Paris: Editions du Seuil, 1966)

Galtier, Roland; Lueders, Kurt. "L'Orgue Cavaillé-Coll (1838) de l'église Notre Dame-de-Lorette à Paris et sa 'Restauration,' " *La Flûte Harmonique* No. IX (April 1979) 4-15.

Gastoué, Amédée. "A Great French Organist, Alexandre Boëly, and His Works," *The Musical Quarterly* XXX/3 (July 1944) 336-44.

Gerig, Reginald R. *Famous Pianists & Their Technique.* (Washington-New York: Luce, 1974).

Giles, Hugh. "The Mysticism of César Franck." Unpublished S.M.M. thesis, Union Theological Seminary, New York City, 1931 (33 pp.).

Gleason, Harold. See Moeser, James.

Goodrich, Wallace. *The Organ in France.* (Boston: The Boston Music Company, 1917)

Guilmant, Alexandre. "La musique d'orgue," *Encyclopédie de la Musique et Dictionnaire du Conservatoire, Deuxième Partie.* (Paris: Delagrave, 1926)

Haag, Herbert. *César Franck als Orgelkomponist.* (Kassel: Bärenreiter, 1936)

Hardouin, Pierre. "Le grand orgue de Saint-Jacques-du-Haut-Pas," *Connaissance de l'orgue* No. 4 (1972) 25–28.

———. *Le Grand Orgue de Notre-Dame-de-Paris.* (Chambray-les-Tours: Bärenreiter, 1973)

Hazard, L. "De l'honnêteté en matière d'édition musicale . . . ," *L'Orgue* LXXXVI/2 (April–June 1958) 38–43. (A critique of the Novello edition of Franck's organ works. Using the *Cantabile* as an example, the author shows the disparity between the English edition and Franck's original indications.)

Hesse, Adolph Friedrich. "Einiges über Orgeln, deren Einrichtung und Behandlung in Österreich, Italien, Frankreich und England," *Neuen Zeitschrift für Musik* (1853) 53 ff.

Hinton, John William. *César Franck: Some Personal Reminiscences.* (London: Reeves, 1912)

Huré, Jean. *L'Esthétique de l'orgue.* (Paris: Senart, 1923)

Imbert, Hughes. "Vincent d'Indy." Translated by Makower in *Studies in Music by Various Authors*, reprinted from *The Musician*, ed. Robin Grey. (London: Simpkin, Marshall, Hamilton, Kent, 1901)

d'Indy, Vincent. *César Franck.* (Paris: Alcan, 1906) Translated by Rosa Newmarch. (London: John Lane The Bodley Head, 1909)

Jaquet, Marie-Louise. "L'oeuvre d'orgue de César Franck et notre temps," *L'Orgue* No. 167 (July–Sept. 1978) 23–24.

Klotz, Hans. "Romantische Registrierkunst, César Franck an der Cavaillé-Coll Orgel," *M. Kirche* XLV/5 (1975) 217–24.

Kooiman, Ewald. "Het Cavaillé-Coll orgel in de Ste. Clotilde in Parijs," *Het Orgel* (July–Aug. 1981) 233–41.

Lamazou, Abbé Pierre Henri. *Étude sur l'orgue monumental de Saint-Sulpice et la facture d'orgue moderne.* (Paris: Repos, [1863])

Landgraf, Armin. *Musica Sacra zwischen Symphonie und Improvisation: César Franck und seine Musik für den Gottesdienst.* (Tutzing: Hans Schneider, 1975)

Langlais, Jean. "Letter to the Editor," Paris, 1 August 1971, *The Diapason* (Sept. 1971) 17. A letter in which the present organist of the Basilica of Sainte-Clotilde elucidates his position as the heir of authentic interpretation of Franck's music.

Lapommeraye, Pierre de. "César Franck Intime. (Une conversation avec M. Gabriel Pierné)," *Le Ménestrel* (1 December 1922) 484–86.

keu, Guillaume. "Lettres inédites," *Courrier musical* (Jan.–Dec. 1906).

Lommens, Jacques-Nicolas. *École d'orgue*. (Bruxelles: Schott, 1862)

Letocart Henri. "Quelques souvenirs II," *L'Orgue*, No. 37 (March 1939) 4-6.

Long Marguerite. *Le Piano*. (Paris: Salabert, 1959)

Lord, Robert Sutherland, "The Sainte-Clotilde Traditions–Franck, Tournemire and Langlais: Conversation and Commentary with Jean Langlais," *The Diapason* (March 1975) 3.

Lhôte, Georges. "Remarks on the French Organ," *ISO-Information* No. 1 (Feb. 1969) 37-82.

Lueders, Kurt. "Amours, Délices et Grandes Orgues, Part V," *Music* X/4 (April 1976) 34-38.

Mahaut, Albert. *Le Chrétien, homme d'action*. (Paris: Édition de Librairie, 1920)

———. *L'OEuvre d'Orgue de César Franck*. (Paris: Chez (Auteur, 1923) This 58 page monograph contains the essay "Souvenirs personnels de son dernier élève," originally published in 1905, and three additional chapters, "L'OEuvre d'Orgue, sa Vulgarisation," an appendix containing reviews of Mahaut's 1898 recitals in which he played, for the first time in history, the complete organ works of Franck, and an "Analyse des Pièces d'Orgue."

Marchal, André. "André Marchal talks to Rodney Baldwyn on the occasion of César Franck's 150th birthday," *Organist's Review* LVIII (Dec. 1973) 11-13.

———. Letter to the author, 18 May 1980.

Massenet, Jules, *Mes Souvenirs*. (Paris: Lafitte, 1912) Translated by H. Villiers Barnett as *My Recollections*. (Boston: Small, Maynard, 1919)

(Merklin). *Liste des Orgues Electroniques de La Maison J. Merklin*. (Paris, 1891)

Miramon Fitz-James, B. de. "La Réinauguration de l'Orgue de Ste.-Clotilde (20 juin 1933)." *L'Orgue*, No. 15 (July-Sept, 1933) 8-9.

Moeser, James. "Harold Gleason Interviewed," *The American Organist*, XV/9 (Sept. 1981) 42-46.

Mohr, Wilhelm. *Caesar Franck*. (Tutzing: Schneider, 1969)

Moreau, Félix. "La restauration du 'Cavaillé-Coll' de La Cathédrale de Luçon," *L'Orgue* No. 133/1 (Jan.-March 1970) 3-8.

Morgan, Florence Alice. "Cyclism in the Works of César Franck." Master's thesis, Columbia University, New York City, 1932.

Ober, William B. "De mortibus musicorum," *Stereo Review* (Nov. 1970) 79-84. (Dr. Ober, a pathologist, has included in this article an account [82-83] of the circumstances surrounding Franck's death.)

O'Daniels, Harold C. "The Harmonium Music of César Franck." S.M.M. thesis, Union Theological Seminary School of Sacred Music, New York City, 1956.

"L'orgue de l'église St.-Hippolyte à Poligny," *La Flûte Harmonique* No. 2, Paris, 1976, 12-14.

Paderewski, Ignace; Lawton, Mary. *The Paderewski Memoirs*. (New York: Scribners, 1938)

Peeters, Flor. *Ars Organi, Pars III*. (Bruxelles: Schott, 1954)

———. Letter to the author, 27 April 1981.

————. "The Organ Works of César Franck," *Music* V/8 (Aug. 1971) 22–27, 40, and V/9 (Sept. 1971) 40–42, 51.

Pierné, Gabriel. See Lapommeraye, Pierre de.

Ply, Abbé H.-J. *La facture moderne etudiée à l'orgue de Saint-Eustache.* (Lyon: Perrin et Marinet, 1878).

Poulenc, Francis. *Emmanuel Chabrier.* (Paris: La Palatine, 1961).

Pruitt, William. "Charles Tournemire and the style of Franck's major organ works," *The Diapason* (Oct. 1970) 17.

Quittard, Henri. "Les Chorals variés pour orgue de César Franck," *La Revue d'histoire et de critique musicale* (1911) 120 ff.

Rapport de la Commission d'expertise de l'orgue de choeur de l'église Sainte-Clotilde à Paris. (Paris: E. Waltelet, 1888).

Raugel, Félix. "Du second au troisième grand orgue de Saint-Étienne-du-Mont," *L'Orgue* No. 90 (April–June 1959) 38–44.

————. *Les Grandes Orgues des Églises de Paris.* (Paris: Librairie Fischbacher, 1927).

————. "The Organs of the Church of Saint-Jacques du Haut-Pas, Paris," *The Organ* X/4 (Oct. 1923) 110–13.

Rayfield, Robert. "Rhythmic conventions in the performance of César Franck's Three Chorals," *Music* IX/6 (June 1975) 29–33.

Riemenschneider, Albert; Keller, Herman. "A Short History of the Basic Griepenkerl Edition of Bach's Organ Works," *Eighth Music Book*, ed. Max Hinrichsen. (London: Hinrichsen, 1956) 137–40.

Rockholt, Preston. "César Franck," *Music* VI/6 (June 1972) 19–23.

Ropartz, Guy de. "César Franck," *Revue Internationale de Musique* (13 June 1898) Translated by Miss Milman in *Studies in Music by Various Authors*, reprinted from *The Musician*, ed. Robin Grey. (London: Simpkin, Marshall, Hamilton, Kent, 1901).

Russell, Carlton T. "Franck's *L'Organiste* Reconsidered," *The American Organist* LIII/2 (Feb. 1970) 9–12. (Corrections to this article appeared in "You the Reader," *The American Organist* LIII/6 (Nov. 1970) 3.

Sabatier, François. *Les aventures du grand orgue de Notre-Dame-de-Paris au XIXe siècle.* Volume I, 1792–1859; Volume II, 1859–1963. (Paris: L'Orgue, Cahiers et Mémoires de l'Orgue, 1974–75).

————. *La Palettte sonore de Cavaillé-Coll.* Paris: Revue "Jeunesse et Orgue," 1979.

Saint-Saëns, Camille. *Les idées de Vincent d'Indy.* (Paris: Lafitte, 1918) Translated by Fred Rothwell and included in Saint-Saëns' *Outspoken Essays on Music.* (Boston: Small, Maynard, 1922).

————. "Music in the Church," *The Musical Quarterly* II/1 (Jan. 1916) 1–8.

————. *Portraits et Souvenirs.* (Paris: Sociéte d'édition artistique, 1899) Translated by Edwin Rich as *Musical Memories.* (Boston: Small, Maynard, 1919).

Schmitt, Georges. "Nouveau Manuel complet de l'Organiste," *Encyclopédie Roret.* (Paris, 1855).

Schouten, Hennie. "De harmonische constructie van het tweede orgelkoraal van César Franck," *De Schalmei* III/9 (5 Sept. 1948) 107-10.

Schweitzer, Albert. "À propos de la Discussion sur la Facture d'Orgues" (1914), *L'Orgue*, Cahiers et Mémories, No. 22 (Paris, 1979) 14-34.

———. *Deutsche und französische Orgelbaukunst und Orgelkunst*. (Leipzig: Breitkopf & Härtel, 1906).

de Serres, Louis. "Quelques souvenirs sur le père Franck, mon maître," *L'Art musical* (Paris, 1936) (29 Nov. 1935)67-69 (6 Dec. 1935) 89-90.

Smith, Rollin. "A Franck Organ Tour," *Music* VI/12 (Dec. 1972) 48-49.

———. "César Franck–The Organist," *The Diapason* (Feb. 1973) 9.

Smith, Ronald. *Alkan: Volume One: The Enigma*. (London: Kahn & Averill, 1976)

Souvenir du 22 octòbre 1904. À César Franck, ses disciples, ses amis, ses admirateurs. (Paris: Cabasson, 1904)

Sumner, William L. "The Organ at Sainte-Clotilde, Paris," *The Organ* XIII/52 (April 1934) 240-44.

Toebosch, Louis. "Misallenia (sic) rondom César Francks orgelwerken," *Het Orgel* (Sept. 1979) 305 ff.

Tournemire, Charles. *César Franck* (Paris: Delagrave, 1931).

———. (An article describing his recording experience.) *L'Intransigeant* (28 April 1930).

———. *Précis d'exécution, de registration et d'improvisation à l'Orgue*. (Paris: Max Eschig, 1936)

Vallas, Léon. "César Franck, élève du Conservatoire de Paris," *Revue Musicale de France*, VI, 1946. (Oct 25 1946) 2-4.

———. *La véritable histoire de César Franck* (Paris: Flammarion, 1950) Translated by Hubert Foss as *César Franck*. (New York: Oxford University Press, 1951)

Vanmackelberg, Maurice. "L'orgue de la cathédrale de Saint-Omer," *L'Orgue* No. 148 (Oct.-Dec. 1973) 152-57.

Vierne, Louis. *Journal*. (Paris: Les Amis de l'Orgue, 1970)

———. *Mes Souvenirs*. (Paris: Les Amis de l'Orgue, 1970) Translated by Esther E. Jones as "Memoirs of Louis Vierne: His Life and Contacts with Famous Men," *The Diapason* (Sept. 1938-Sept. 1939) (Note: Originally published in a series of articles in *L'Orgue* from Sept. 1934 to Sept. 1937.)

Vivet, Arment. "Eugène Gigout," L'Orgue et les Organistes, No. 23 (15 Feb. 1926) 25-28.

Waters, Clarence. "Letter to the Editor," *The Diapason* (June 1971) 15. (A student of Marcel Dupré defines his teacher's Franck tradition.)

White, Ernest. *Lectures on Franck's* Trois Chorals *and Bach's* Orgelbüchlein. (New York: Privately printed, 1938)

White, Robert W. "Franck and the 8 ft.-less Organ," *The Diapason* (June 1962) 8.

Whitworth, Reginald. "The standard console of Aristide Cavaillé-Coll," *The Rotunda* II/3 (Sept. 1928) 18-20.

Widor, Charles Marie. "La Classe d'Orgue du Conservatoire," *Le Ménestrel* (3 June 1921) 237-38.

————. "Preface," *L'orgue de J. S. Bach* by André Pirro. (Paris: Fischbacher, 1895) Translated by Wallace Goodrich as *Johann Sebastian Bach, the Organist.* (New York: Schirmer, 1902)

INDEX